RISE UP

Growth of Women's Sports Officiating Basketball, Living with a Chronic Illness

Dana H. Senders

Rise up
Growth of Women's Sports Officiating Basketball,
Living with a Chronic Illness

Copyright © 2018 by Dana H. Senders
Edited by Alex Dankers

Although every precaution has been taken to verify the accuracy of the information contained herein, the author and publisher assume no responsibility for any errors or omissions. No liability is assumed for damages that may result from the use of information contained within.

Library of Congress Control Number: 2017964749
ISBN-13: Paperback: 978-1-64151-411-8
    PDF: 978-1-64151-413-2
    Epub: 978-1-64151-414-9
    Kindle: 978-1-64151-415-6
    Hardcover: 978-1-64151-412-5

Printed in the United States of America

LitFire LLC
1-800-511-9787
www.litfirepublishing.com
order@litfirepublishing.com

MW,
I couldn't have done this without your loving support.

Contents

FOREWORD

Chris Gobrecht ~ Women's Basketball Head Coast, United States Air Force Academy

Very few people have had or will have the sense of fulfillment that comes with knowing you were there for some of the most formative and transformative years in the history of something that you chose for your life's work. I often said that the advancement of women in society, business, government, and all professional fields, was reflected for the world to see, in the ever-increasing success and accomplishments of the female athlete. Those of us involved in the sport of women's basketball in the 1980's and 1990's got a front row seat to history. However, the fulfillment comes from knowing we weren't just spectators; we were players on that stage, and we were part of making history.

Dana and I got to be leaders in our fields at a time when women were not doing our jobs that often. We had to do it well or it would be that much harder for the women coming after us to get the same opportunity. We proved that women will compete as hard as men and with every bit as much intensity; maybe more! It might have been strange to some to see the kind of intense confrontation between coaches and officials that is common for men now happening between women or between women and men. We were the lucky ones.

We never know how high we can go until we rise.

It's hard to believe that at 17 years old I had no idea where my life would turn with a comment to some basketball referees. I'm so grateful to those referees because of where my life followed after that moment. I'm grateful for all the people I've met on the way. I believe that as I went through the next 35 plus years that the whole time I acted like I had been there before!

CHAPTER 1
My Journey

This was the start of my journey through basketball, officiating, and multiple sclerosis. I was about 12 years old when I started playing basketball.

There were six players at this time in women's basketball: two in the front court, two in the back, and two rovers that could go anywhere on the floor. I was a rover. That's where it started. This was before Title IX passed which help create equality for women in sports.

Through self-reflection, I think my goal was to please my parents. Sports made my parents happy and I was good at them. My mother had rheumatoid arthritis that kept her away from her doing any sports I tried soccer, but in the first week I sprained my ankle. I attempted running different track events, but my ankle pain kept coming back. I liked volleyball, but I wasn't very good at it, so I only played in high school. When I was seventeen, I had surgery on my left ankle because it kept spraining. Those sprains have been bothering me ever since I was a teenager.

My ankles kept spraining and the ligaments kept stretching. In those days, they took those ligaments out, drilled a hole in the bone, and rerouted tendons to take the place of ligaments. The foot I had this surgery on is the same foot that broke while I was officiating in 1995.

I was looking for unconditional love through sports. It drove me to be the best at everything that I tried to do. I found success in softball and officiating, but I still don't think I found what I was looking for and I don't know if I can ever reach that goal. I guess it never stopped making me feel better. It truly seems to be what I've been missing all my life.

I think this all started as a kid I've been looking for my parent's approval. I don't know why unconditional love from my parents was my goal because I'm sure they gave it to me, but I guess I never felt it. As an adult, I never seem to get it. Both my parents have now passed now however maybe this is psychoanalyzing my success too much, but I'm sure this is part of what drove me.

When I was younger, I learned how to play tennis, ski, and dance from my dad. I always tried my best and get trophies to show my parents how good I was. When I was 16 years old I started teaching tennis because of everything that I learned from my dad. In 1973, the minimum wage was a $1.60 and it only cost $5 to fill up a gas tank. Working at that age helped develop my ethics and started me down the path of teaching.

Roger Senders ~ Brother

Dana is a champion! Whether winning the national championship in fast pitch softball as a teen, winning first chair in the clarinet section in high school band, or being in the vanguard of women refereeing college sports, Dana has always wanted and strived to be the best.

I have known Dana since birth, her birth at least. As her two-year older brother, I wonder if Dana didn't feel in my shadow. I certainly felt in hers although I don't think Dana realized it. Writing this has gotten me to think about our youth. I won awards. She strived and succeeded in winning more. I did well academically. She did also but I think I did better in that arena. Yes. I'm competitive too! She certainly did better athletically. Let's just say that I may be better at hand-eye coordination, but she has me hands down with the rest of our bodies (and maybe, just maybe the hand-eye coordination as well). You don't get to be a national champion or a multi-sport all-star like Dana did unless you're really, really committed, skilled, disciplined and driven, all adjectives that aptly describe Dana.

Dana works hard in everything she does. She is proud and has a strong will that serves her well. Occasionally, her pride or commitment gets in her way of achieving all that I think she might. On the flip side, her drive and occasional bull-headed focus on achieving her goal has set her apart by succeeding in places where women often didn't.

I've always been proud of Dana, as an athlete, a musician, a pioneer women official, the teacher and leader of referees in two college conferences and an individual who has fought and continues to fight her physical challenges tooth and nail!

Like most, Dana and I were sibling rivals in our youth. That competition drove both of us. Even then and certainly today, I have always and continue to respect her, be impressed by her and be proud that she is my sister.

CHAPTER 2

Start Officiating

My path to officiating started in 1975 at Mercer Island High School. I played varsity basketball as a senior. My dad always yelled at the referees at the games, and I took that behavior with me and yelled at referees too. The two referees for the game, Toni Turnbull and Barbie Yamauchi, came over to the bench during time out. They told me that if I didn't like their calls, then why don't I ref myself. I didn't know at the time, but they started my next thirty-five years in basketball officiating.

I went to Western Washington University, after graduation, although at that time it was still called a college. I chose Western because it was far enough from home for some space, but close enough that I could still return home if I needed to. At that time, WWU cost $300 per quarter, a small amount compared to education today.

While picking my classes, I noticed basketball officiating. I didn't know the teacher was Lynda Goodrich, so I found out during class that Lynda was also the basketball coach. I tried out for the team, despite my short height, but back in 1975, 5'4" wasn't that short for basketball. I made the junior varsity team. I loved playing, but knew I wasn't very good. Officiating sparked my passion.

Lynda Goodrich ~ Mentor, Teacher, Coach:

Dana took a class from me at WWU, Officiating Basketball, it was a class designed to teach students the way to officiate basketball, signals, court positioning, areas of responsibility, dealing with players and coaches, professional approach and of course the rules and interpretation. Dana was a student who took to officiating like a "duck to water".

She grasped the nuances of officiating, had a great court presence and an assertive way of calling without being over assertive. Dana went on to call high school, college games. Her reputation among officials, coaches was of high respect. She became an official a coach wanted on their game (I speak from experience) because you knew she would be impartial, call a great game and never have to question. She eventually became the supervisor of officials, when her health kept her from calling the game, she was able to lend her expertise to developing young officials, supervise officials and help them become better. She was always willing to listen and try to make situations better. Her impact on women's basketball, especially in the northwest, will always be remembered.

During my first year in college, referees wore blue and white striped shirts. I was working a game at Shorewood High School and the zipper broke on my pants. I tried to pull down my shirt to cover the zipper because those shirts did not tuck in at that time because of a blue waist band. I held the shirt down until halftime. During half-time, I knew I needed to find my partner. If they had a safety pin, I could last for the second half. I found a pin, pinned my pants, still keeping the shirt over my zipper, and went back out on the floor. Our colors starting as blue and white stripes meaning that, with my small feet, it was easy to match my uniform with the regulation white tennis shoes. But then when our colors switched to black and white stripes, I needed black shoes. Very few places made black shoes small enough to fit my feet. I wore a size 5 men's shoe to get by. There are now supportive shoes for women and shoes with a wide range of sizes, but back then, we had to take what we could get. I think that officials today hate when shoes don't fit, but most of us in the seventies and early eighties couldn't even find shoes, so we figured out a way to get business done.

On the first day of my sophomore year of college I goofed around with some friends outside of my dorms, I jumped against my friends back, slid off her down jacket, and I fell off hitting my head on the ground. I felt a pop in my back. My friend's mother came over when she heard me yelling in pain. She was a nurse, and knew to touch my foot, asking me if I had any feeling in my foot to check for spine injuries. She called an ambulance, and I took a ride over to the hospital. I sprained muscles in my lower back, and called my parents, but being tough was all I knew. I told them not to come.

When I returned from the hospital, I could barely walk, so trying out for basketball was out of the question. I needed a friend to help me just to reach the bathroom. I missed the first week of tryouts. I tried out during week two, but I still couldn't run well. The coach said we had to keep working running "Z" until someone quit, and my teammates encouraged me to stop because I had an excuse to quit, but I would not be the first to stop. I ended up on junior varsity that year, but I discovered I loved officiating more than playing.

After my sophomore year, I played fast-pitch softball on a team from Everett, Washington. While playing a tournament in Portland, Oregon, one of my friends suggested I go to Oregon State for school. Out of state tuition was very expensive, but Western Washington didn't have a softball program, so when Oregon State offered a partial scholarship, I decided to go to Oregon. I practiced over fall for the spring softball season in the Pacific Northwest rain. We practiced in the field house to avoid the rain and threw long distance in the field house before warming up our shoulders and arms. I had a slight pain in my right shoulder, but I didn't care. I was 20 and loved being on the team. So I kept playing. When the pain grew serious, I finally went to a doctor. He said I had tendonitis and bursitis in my arm and needed to stop playing.

Games hadn't started yet, and my left shoulder started to hurt. I was throwing again with my right arm in pain, but I really wanted to play. I went back to the doctor's office to find out I had tendonitis and bursitis in my left shoulder as well.

I kept playing, putting my right arm in serious pain. The doctor put me in a sling for 3 weeks. There was nothing I could do except sit and watch. Coach Rita expected me to be positive, even though I wasn't playing. I had a tough time rooting for my team from the bench. Coach called me into her office and told me I needed to change my attitude about playing or we would have a problem, I think at the time not being able to play frustrated me.

I found out later that my coach was afraid I would sue if she put me in the game too soon, even though the thought never crossed my mind. She called me into her office again and told me that if I didn't care anymore, as my lack of enthusiasm from the bench suggested, I would be cut from the team. So I left. I decided to return to Western Washington for my senior year.

The bursitis and tendonitis followed me years later. I walked with a cane because of MS and fell with my right arm pointed straight at the ground. The MRI of my shoulder showed a torn rotator cuff. The doctor said he could try and repair it, but there was only a 50% guarantee of total reparation. I used my left arm more to compensate, but I tore the rotator cuff in that shoulder as well. As time went on, I tore my bicep tendon in my right arm and two out of four tendons in my rotator cuff completely with a third partial tear. The only answer that I could come up with to help was cortisone shots to alleviate the pain. I started getting cortisone into my shoulders because I used my arms so much, transferring pressure from my legs to my arms because my legs stopped getting the message from MS nerve damage. Cortisone shots help for the pain, but I can only get them every 4 months. It works for a while so I can still use my arms to transfer myself. The tears in my shoulders and my bicep tendon are pains I live with. What pains me more is emotional frustration from needing help. I don't stand anymore, the pain lingering from sophomore year. To this day, I don't think many people know how bad my shoulders are, except maybe my doctors

I had a tough time living in Corvallis around redneck conservatives. After one year there, I returned to Western Washington to for my fourth year. I lived with my parents for my first quarter, working in Seattle.

The Bellingham officiating crew loved me, so they brought me back in January. I was older than most of the players on the junior varsity team. I tried out for the basketball team at Western, my senior year because I wanted to play for varsity. Lynda Goodrich called me into her office after tryouts, telling me I would make the varsity team, but only as the twelfth player on a twelve-person roster. I wouldn't see much playing time, so Lynda asked if I would coach the JV team instead. Our JV coach passed away from a heart attack at the age of 22, so the team needed a coach. I knew I didn't want to be the twelfth player on the varsity team, so I agreed to coaching JV. That year we went 13 and 3 and I loved every second of coaching. I no longer missed playing basketball, so I decided to stick with coaching.

CHAPTER 3
Softball

At Western Washington University the senior year before graduation, I created a softball club because Western didn't have a team. Since I started it, I decided that I would coach because I couldn't play with my shoulders. We had a tournament in May over in Yakima, Washington.

Unfortunately, that was on May 18, 1980. While we were warming up for our first game an announcement came over the loudspeaker that everyone needed to go to their cars. We headed to our cars when we saw white flecks coming down from the sky. We later found out that it was volcanic ash from the Mount Saint Helens eruption.

We made it to our cars and the daytime turned pitch black from the ash. We decided as a team to head to Denny's, in light of the game's sudden cancellation. In the darkness, we could see the light from the Denny's. Off to Denny's we went with two cars. We got separated because one of the girls had family in Yakima, so we called her father to ask where to go and what to do. I was 22 years old and still in college, so I wasn't sure where to go. We followed him up to his house. Fourteen of us all piled into their house and, we later learned that all of the freeways out of Yakima were closed. There are really only two freeways out, so we were stranded in the house. The day went on and it was still pitch-black going into the night. The fourteen of us had to fit in the house and, in retrospect, I don't know how we all fit. I was the coach, so I went to 7-11 with my player's father, because that was pretty much the only store that was open at that time. I purchased all of the canned soup, vegetables, and fruit we could put into a basket and brought it back to the house. We ended up having to stay there for three days, the length needed to clear up the freeways. Because of the eruption, we couldn't get to our finals at Western Washington University, so I had to call the school and talk to the athletic director to let all of our classes know we were stuck.

The freeways did open up, but they would only let one car pass through at a time. We were all lined up, moving one car length every 30 seconds. So, instead of keeping the car running, we decided to push both cars every 30 seconds. This went on for about two miles until we got our turn at the front of the line. We were all wearing masks, kind of like surgical masks, because the ash was floating through the air and we didn't want to inhale it. It took 2 hours for us to get to the front of the line so we could go over the pass. This experience taught us compromise: we figured out where to stay, where to sleep, how to move the car, and, as the leader, I needed to set an example of what we were going to do. We were an amazing team despite never playing one inning in Yakima. Despite knowing nothing about our predicament, I had to act like I had been there before.

CHAPTER 4

Coaching

I started my coaching job at Edmonds Community College as the softball coach. I coached for two years at Shoreline Community College before, the job at Edmonds seemed to be a better fit for me, so I took the job there.

That season, while I was buying some equipment for the softball team, I asked the manager at 3GI athletics if they had any job openings. They hired me on the spot. This job put me in the sales world for the rest of my adult life.

I worked as a basketball official as well as at 3GI in the early eighties. During this time, I officiated a junior college game in Tacoma, Washington. It was cold outside without much precipitation, so I didn't think too much about it. I arrived at the gym at about 5:30 and went in. When I came out after the game at 9pm, there was 8 inches of snow on the ground, an unusual amount for Tacoma. I cleaned the snow from the windows on my little red Honda. I was there with a friend of mine so we got in the car, got on the freeway, and traffic moved slowly. Rather than crawl through traffic, I took the next exit by the Tacoma Dome, saw a hotel, and got a room. A concert at the Tacoma Dome was canceled due to the weather, so when I came downstairs to get something to eat I saw hundreds of people in the lobby sleeping on the chairs or whatever they could find out to lay down on.

In the morning, we put chains on the car tires got on the freeway and headed towards Edmonds my home. After we started on the freeway going fairly slow I counted the cars that were stopped on the road. By the time I got to my house, I counted 30 cars parked on the freeway, some in the lanes and some to the side of the road. I wonder where the driver went after abandoning their cars.

I tried to turn the expenses to my supervisor at the time. He chuckled and said we didn't have money for a hotel room. I earned $90 from the game and over $100 for the room, but stopping for a hotel was still one of the better decisions I made in my 35 years in the officiating world. This game was on Saturday night, so I had Sunday to recover and wait to go to work at 3GI the next day.

CHAPTER 5

Pay for Women's Sports

I was coaching softball at the Community College level at Edmonds Community College. At the time, the stipend for the women's coach was $750 while it was $3,000 for the men's baseball coach, a big difference but I decided to take the coaching job anyway and make the best of it. I only had 9 players, the minimum you need for fast-pitch, but we played well and got through the season to our next year

This year, I had a full 12 players, and most of them were very good including an great pitcher, so I decided to take them on a road trip. I rented a Winnebago and started driving. I set up double headers in Ashland, Oregon; Redding, California; and Reno, Nevada. My assistant coach was supposed to go with me, but she later decided not to go. I took the kids anyway because I promised them, and I could depend on the oldest to drive part of the way. So we went off on the road trip arriving at southern Oregon early in the morning.

I drove the whole way before check-in when we arrived at the hotel room. I caught the flu so, even though I was responsible for these 18 to 19-year olds, they were on their own for part of the trip. I went to sleep to rest for our afternoon game. I felt slightly better, so I went to the playing field that afternoon. We played outside of Ashland the next day after playing morning game. We won both games and were back on the road, heading towards Redding.

One of my player's grandparents lived in Redding, so we stopped at their home. Some of the kids stayed inside to while I slept in the Winnebago, and we drove to Reno in the morning. We got to Reno and checked into the hotel. The kids had a curfew, being all under 21, so I was thinking they couldn't get into that much trouble. I was the only adult supervising and I told them there would be a bed check. So I went around to the rooms to do a bed check to find one of the rooms completely empty and two players in another room missing. The remaining kids gave in and told me where the others were. One of the older ones I found felt the brunt of my anger. I sent all the other players back to their rooms and had a long chat with this older player on the team.

One of my favorite Danaisms is act like you've been there before. New officials, when doing higher level games, would be nervous, but if you believe like you've been there before, nobody will even question that you're new. I was really put into the "act like you've been there before" mindset here because I never had to supervise people this closely before. Despite my inexperience, I needed to figure it out and work through and balance disciplining my team while handling the awkward environment the next day. We got up, took the 30-minute drive to the college where we were playing our games, and I told the players they could make no noise. No talking, no music, no nothing. They had to think about what they put everybody through the night before.

At the next college, some players stayed in dorm rooms and some stayed in the Winnebago. We played our first game and won. So I thought I handled the night before well and it translated into a successful game. I was in the Winnebago with some of the team when I heard knock on the door. A security guy asked who was in charge. I said it's me. The guard found students in the dorms drinking.

I'm beyond furious. I go to the dorms and send everybody back to their own rooms, and just don't know what to do because this was another situation where I hadn't done it before. The kids knew I was upset. We played six games and I thought that I could rely on the oldest player to drive, but I didn't know what to do anymore and decided to drive the whole way instead. We were on our way to Spokane to work our first time in the community college conference that we were in. We got to the hotel in Spokane to rest for the games the next day. We played a double header and lost both games. We were dog-tired. I had talked to only teens for the last six days and felt like talking to an adult, so I called my boss in Seattle and told her I just need to talk to a grown-up. I was tired of being responsible for irresponsible kids.

Overall though, they did pretty well. It was as much a learning experience for me as it was for them. We headed back to Seattle, tired. We returned the Winnebago, making a deal with the rental company since we were college students. I had all the kids stay and help with the cleanup. I feel this Winnebago trip had to be the longest week of my life, but I didn't know any better than to do it. I felt up to doing it again, but I needed a lot of recovery. It was a full week of acting like I had been there before. I really learned responsibility at this young age.

CHAPTER 6
Playing Softball

I loved softball. We didn't have softball in high school, but I participated in summer league fast-pitch softball and, eventually, I moved onto women's slow pitch softball.

One of my proudest moments was at a national slow pitch softball tournament in LA. We were a competitive team and that was the best game I've ever played. My batting average for the tournament was 750 and we were in the middle of a 64-team tournament. It was the last day, and we were still in the winner's bracket. The score was tied. I played in right-center field, and they had the bases loaded with only one out. They just needed to score one run to win. As an outfielder, I had to catch a ball, but we needed to throw it home to get them out. I wasn't that deep in the outfield due to my fading shoulder strength when the batter hit a line drive into outfield. I moved close enough for a diving catch, the runners started to move thinking it was a base hit, but I threw it to first to get a double play once I made the catch.

Then I got up to bat, got a hit, and scored the winning run. We ended up getting fourth in the nation for that tournament, and I was an all-star for hitting. In my entire softball career, that was the only time our team came together and played that well. It was okay that we didn't win the tournament because that one game is enough to keep me warm.

In general, what I liked about softball was being good at a team sport. I had more fun playing softball than other sports. I loved being outside and playing in the sunshine. I especially enjoyed sliding headfirst into bases, just like Pete Rose, to the point that my brother called me "Rita Rose". I was not a home run hitter by any means, but I could hit singles and hit the ball right where the infielders weren't. I enjoyed outsmarting the other team. I tried to play sports mostly by with my head because I wasn't that physically talented. This mindset translated well into officiating.

When I coached softball, I would tell the young athletes to think before they did things and to use their heads. If you have to move in or take an extra base away do it. You have to think when you're playing and you have to know what you're doing, ahead of time. You have to play the odds. If you make a specific move, you need to think ahead to what their best reaction is and how to respond to this reaction. I succeeded because I thought ahead.

I started in the outfield, hurt my shoulder and couldn't make those long throws anymore, moved to second base, to pitcher, and then to coaching.

CHAPTER 7

Women Officials in the 80's

I remember in the mid-eighties, a few students heckled me during a junior college game where the gyms are quite a bit smaller. One student yelled 'go back to Lady Foot Locker'. One told me to 'go back to the kitchen'. I didn't like those moments, but, in reflection, those comments show how few women refereed basketball games in the eighties. I shook those comments off during my career, but, thankfully, I didn't hear too many of them.

A big change in basketball over time has been the size of gyms, the size of the women's ball, and crowds attending games. I refereed in smaller gyms throughout my entire refereeing career. The gyms in the West Coast Conference just didn't drive many people to the smaller gyms. I'm grateful that I worked in those conferences, but I could hear everything that was yelled from the stands. Crowds now are so much bigger, facilities are bigger to fit the crowds and for the officials, and the atmosphere is much better. Everybody should know the progress in culture from between when I officiated in the eighties and the early nineties and now. When I started playing basketball in 1975, the basketball has gotten smaller for women. With my small hands, that would have been great in college. I'm sure it's great for the players now.

I didn't like to play basketball much because I wasn't skilled, and I was only 5'4". What I love about officiating is thinking ahead. That's what makes a successful official, just like playing softball. As an official, you can predict what the plays are going to be, how to make the right call for each play, and knowing when a play is legal or illegal. I never felt too short in stature to officials, coaches, or anybody. Even when I couldn't walk anymore, I never felt short. I think the minute you start thinking anyone is bigger or taller, you're giving some of your power away.

I officiated a game in Tacoma at the University of Puget Sound. I was the under the basket when a girl went up to take a shot. The defensive player was going to swat, and I was sure she was going to foul her. I blew my whistle and the defensive player came down with the ball without contact. "You're not going to call a foul?" I said no I am not!

This is the only time I ever did this: I went up to the coach and apologized, explaining my error and saying that was not a foul. The coach told me not to do it again.

Communication is the biggest thing in officiating. If you can do that you can be successful. This translated to my officiating camps I eventually ran. To be a good official and to be a woman in officiating, you have to find some way to be better, make your calls, and communicate to the coaches. I have at least 100 stories of different conversations with coaches and their respect for my calls, and a skill to talk to probably 8 different division one coaches to this day.

I always taught officials to use their voice. "Use your voice!" That's the biggest Danaism I used all the time. If communicating is the most important part of being an official, then your voice is your most important tool.

After officiating small college games, I went straight home so I could make it to work in the morning. Going out at night was not part of my normal ritual. I went dancing after my UW games as my one exception to this rule because I love to dance, and my UW games were usually on Saturday, so I didn't have to work the next day.

I would go line dancing or to the club often enough that my nickname became Disco Dana. Occasionally at the club, people would say they saw me referee the game and that I did a good job. At first, I worried about what they would say to me in the club, but I realized that the recognition was a compliment.

CHAPTER 8

Men Partners

I had a game up at Simon Fraser University in the eighties. This is where I met a lifelong partner, Bill Crowley. We hit it off right away, I think because we were the same height. Bill was the best partner a person could ask for. We were in a gym that I'd never been to, went out to work the game, and it felt great to have a partner support somebody who had never even been to that gym.

Bill was a Canadian official and he helped me meet one of my fantastic camp staff members at one of his camps. He became supervisor of officials in Canada, and his friendship was important to me. I always told him he was my "brother from another mother". Bill felt like family. I don't talk to him that often anymore, but I am grateful he was in my life. He was a excellent official, and from what I know a great supervisor. He was a male partner that truly treated me as an equal.

I was working a game at UW with Marla Denham, the first woman that I worked with in division one. She told me she didn't call many fouls during games. She wanted me to be prepared. I thought this was unusual, but the game went quickly and we did a great job. In the regular season, I didn't work with another woman partner. In the post-season, however, I worked with a few other women including Becky Marshall, the assignor for Division one out of Texas.

In my division one NCAA tournament play, I did not work with another woman. I worked solely with men and made it to the elite eight in division one. When I worked in division two, division three, and community colleges, however, I worked with some women partners. But not many.

The best part about working with another woman at a game was starting our pregame together in the locker room and having that time to communicate. Trust me, two different locker rooms to dress in left us me ill-equipped at many colleges.

For instance, once I was working a community college game with a male partner, and we dressed in separate dressing rooms. As I was heading to my car, I was stopped by some male students who began calling me names and calling me a terrible referee. My partner was still in the locker room and I needed to leave by myself. A somewhat scary moment in my officiating career.

CHAPTER 9

My Vocation

I started work at 3GI's from 8am to 2pm, then I worked from 3pm to 5pm at Edmonds community college as a coach. The best part of 3GI's was becoming the footwear buyer for the store. I did get several free pairs of shoes because I had the same size feet as the sample shoes. However, 3GI's paid wage was only $7 an hour and they had no money in the budget for a raise despite me working six years there. I enjoyed working at 3GI and it worked well with my coaching schedule I needed to look somewhere where I could have an advancement and make more money.

A job opened up at the Olympic Sports with many stores in the northwest. I applied to become the footwear buyer there, but I was hired on to work team sales instead. I believe my wages were around $9 an hour, and I was doing pretty well working in team sports for them.

The owner of the Olympic Sports had their 22-year-old son in charge of the team sales, and he didn't know anything about team sales while I knew a lot about the job. We didn't get along because he tried to boss me around, and, eventually, I was called into the owner's office. The owner told me I either needed to change my attitude about business with his son or leave. I left his office without a job.

I quit Olympic Sports that morning and by the afternoon I was interviewing for a competing sporting goods chain, Athletic Supply. I hadn't signed a no-compete clause with Olympic Sports, so I could keep my accounts from Olympic Sports. I worked at Athletic Supply for two years, but I really couldn't work to my fullest potential because I couldn't sell to my customers, since some of their salesmen were already assigned those accounts. I wanted to succeed in every job I had, so having these obstacles stressed me out.

I found another job in an advertisement for a sports apparel store and I had a lot of experience doing this, so I faxed them my resume and was hired. I loved working for this company because I had my own leads and I did well. So after four years with that company, it was purchased by another apparel company about two minutes away from my home. The owner was very flexible to give me whatever I needed because I was the top salesperson, so I worked for him for three years He started getting frustrated because I wasn't very good at paperwork, and, I admit, that was a problem. When I came in first thing in the morning, he would have a note for me about mistakes in my paperwork. I didn't do everything as I should have, but I asked if he could give me an hour before he gave me notes now. His answered, "I sign your checks, I will communicate to you any way I want to." I managed to stay another year getting these notes. I was making quite a bit of money there, but I wasn't thinking about the money. I found an ad for a store selling novelty items, so I went ahead and kept changing jobs looking for one I liked.

CHAPTER 10
First Camps

My first year at Bob Olson's camp, we drove down from Seattle to Portland and then rode with Bob from Portland to Santa Clara, picking up other officials on the way. We did stop to play golf on the way. Once we arrived at camp, Larry Shepard and Bob Olson both said that they knew I was going to go far. I learned how to use my attitude and my communication skills to my benefit rather than against me and, at the next game at camp, Larry watched me closely. My skills in that game helped me get hired onto the West Coast Conference. I had already been hired in the Pac-10. Dean Crowley, the supervisor, observed one of my games at camp, came up to me, and asked if I was willing to drive to Spokane and work for only $90 an entire game without per diem expenses. Times have changed a lot, but back then, a little money in my pocket and driving all the way to Gonzaga was worth it. To be honest, I would have worked for free. After subtracting gas and food on the road, I made about $20 and it was worth every penny.

I really cannot explain how grateful and excited I was to work division one games. It was only my second year and 36 of my 60 games were at the highest level! I was perhaps the only official from the northwest with that many games on all levels ranging from high school to division one. I ended up giving up high school games because I had trouble officiating at that level. My emotions ranged from sadness to jubilation because it meant I refereed all games like college games now while the kids were not talented enough at that level because I officiated it like a college game.

Officiating was different at that time. The dollar amount per game and travelling was very different pre-9/11. No convenient cell phones. iPhones were years away. Only two people working games in division one and all levels. You needed a corded phone in your car to communicate with other officials when on the road. Division one games were Thursday Saturday with occasional Sunday. The WCC never played on Sunday because of religious reasons

CHAPTER 11

High School Championship

It was my first high school state championship game. I was the only woman in a group of eight referees. Our locker rooms were connected, so my locker room was in the back, and I needed to walk through the men's locker room to get there. I had to yell "women in the room" as i walked through. During this tournament, one of the coaches gave me a score of 0 out of 25 while my partner got a score of 23. The coaches from every game would turn in a score with the observer. The head of officials told me what. That coach had done. I was the first woman referee he'd ever seen on a game. I made it to the championship game that year, while the coach that gave me a 0 was not in the championship!

I worked the state championships in 1988, 1989, and 1990, but I stopped working high school, so I couldn't work anymore state tournaments. Being the first woman at the state tournament and working 3 state championship finals games is a great mark on my career in the northwest. I just started working division one in 1989, so the high school championships fit together to make this a great door opening for me. This was an important starting point for women in 1988, and I kept on going to work many state championships and NCAA tournament games.

CHAPTER 12
Division One Official

My first year officiating basketball for the West Coast Conference, I got paid $90 a game with no per diem. So the only games I worked were University of Portland and Gonzaga University. Women's games are at 5:15pm, so I drove to Spokane and drove home after each game. The second year I would get $120 per game plus per diem. At that time, the schools personally gave us checks at the end of each game. It didn't stop me cashing the check as quickly as I could but later on the schools paid the conference and then the conference paid the officials.

When I travelled mostly by myself, to Portland and Spokane for the WCC, and Oregon schools in the PAC 10, I would stop to get fast-food to eat on the way home. I couldn't really eat before my games because my stomach couldn't handle that. When I think about it now, I am surprised I wasn't 300 pounds with how poor my diet was, but luckily, I was refereeing games to keep myself from gaining weight. I've been told that on a two-person crew each official runs about 5 miles per game. Hopefully now officials are better about making healthy eating decisions.

I really never went out to eat with my partners after games. I had one game in Olympia with Larry Luke, and he was driving and said we're stopping to eat on the way back. So since he was driving I didn't have anything to say about it and we stopped in Chinatown at his favorite Chinese restaurant. The food was great but I didn't get home till 11pm and I had to get up at 6:30 go to work the next day. However, when your partner insists you need to stop, you stop.

Since I've become disabled, with my MS symptoms, I can no longer run my way out of eating poor food. I'm stuck between a rock and a hard place since I've been diagnosed with Celiac disease, a wheat allergy. I wish I knew back then how my dining choices would impact my future. That falls right into the Shoulda, Coulda, Woulda category that I think about often.

CHAPTER 13

Seattle Mariners Grounds Crew

In 1987, I was offered a job doing grounds crew for the Seattle Mariners one spring. My friend got me hired. She was the first woman to work grounds so I was the second. It was in the King Dome after my job at 3GI. I got dressed in the grounds crew uniform and went to help with the setup of the game. I worked there when Ken Griffey Jr., Alvin Davis, and Harold Reynolds played. I was sitting in the Bullpen during the game and the guys out there were bored. One of them asked me what the size my hat was. I took it off to check and he spit seeds in it. I guess that proves they're just little boys in big boy uniforms.

I worked there when baseballs were still not to be given out. I grabbed a couple and got a Ken Griffey Jr. signature. Unfortunately, I gave away both of them to my boss' son. I also found a $100 gift certificate while sweeping during the 7th inning stretch. It belonged to one of the coaches of the Cleveland Indians and they left it behind when changing his pants after sitting in gum. I went to the dugout and gave it back to him. After the game, he told me I could use the certificate more than him, so he gave it to me. Being honest paid off. I went to Sears, bought a watch, and got the rest in cash. I loved working for the Seattle Mariners. I'm still a Mariners fan and this job also included working for the Seattle Seahawks. I was one of the net people so anytime a ball was kicked to the end zone, I would be there to pull the nets up. There were only two of us so we ran back and forth from end-to-end when needed. I'm still a great Seattle Seahawk fan as well. I got to meet Steve Largent and Jim Zorn, but I never got any autographs. I was there for the experience over the two years. Getting to meet those guys was a very special part of my life because it added to the experiences over the years and made me feel closer to the teams I love.

CHAPTER 14

Pac 10 Officiating

In 1989, one of my big story is my first year in the pac-10 I was at the camp for the pac and I was thinking I knew everything about officiating 2 person crew but at the camp the staff members were telling me different things and Carter Rankin was one of the staff and after I'd been told the stand one place he told me to stand another place. So immediately ran to ray DalPagetto the supervisor he was disagreeing with the way he wanted to have it done. So I was walking out the hall and Ray stop me grab my shirt push me up against the wall and told me to stop being that I knew it all or don't let the door hit me on the way out. So I sat down in the hall and tears were coming to my eyes and one of the other officials that she came by and saw me crying and said what's wrong. I told her I thought I was going to quit I couldn't take the way I was being treated. And what she said to me changed my life because she said you can't quit you're the future of women in officiating. So I thought about what she said and I'm so glad that I didn't quit in my life continued and being a great official in the pac and this is when ray only gave me one game and it was the last regular game in the season better than none!

My first Pac-10 game was at Washington State, and it was the last game of the regular season. I waited all year to have my first game in the PAC-10, making it a very long season. I was also invited to the Community College championship tournament in Walla Walla, Washington, but there was a bit of overlap between the games. My game at Washington State was in Pullman, about 70 miles away from Walla Walla, so I could leave the Community College tournament in the middle to go do my division one game. I needed to take one of the small "cigar" planes—the planes with one seat on either side—over to Pullman from Walla Walla.

There were eight officials at the Community College Tournament: seven men and me. The tournament would not provide money for me to get a single room. This was against the law, but it was my first year in division one and I didn't want to make waves. The one single guy of the seven men was the only choice to room with me. It would have been fine except these guys went out to drink one night and he came back to the room and sat on my bed. I just said damn what the heck are you doing go over to your bed. He said I just wanted to talk to you. I told him to get off my bed and go to your bed. The next day, I flew off to Pullman. Again, this isn't an uncommon story for women officials back in the 80's when I started working division one.

I met my partner in Pullman for the game. Three of my friends, including one of my best friends Deb Holemen, drove over from Seattle to bring me back after the game. There was only one locker room for officials. I went out in the hall while my partner dressed. I didn't know at the time that this wasn't any different for any woman official, so I went with the flow. Harold Rhodes was the coach at Washington State for that game and I believe they were playing Oregon.

The game went well and there were observers for the Pac-10 at the game. Here was my first game at Washington State and it was a one-point game with Washington State ahead. I was the lead official and the Oregon player got fouled on her way to the basket at the game being at point nine tenths of a second left on the clock. It was what I call a "God and country call", a call so obvious to make that it was easy to make for me. The kid still had to make the free throws to win the game which she did and the coach from Washington State never said anything. He saw the foul and the game finished with Oregon winning the game. My partner and I met with an observer in the locker room, my first experience with an observer. I sat still while he talked to my partner. He never looked at me or talked to me. In the mail a few days later, I got the written observation from my supervisor. He didn't have much to say about me in the observation. I could tell I was nervous. I wish I still had that observation, so I could show all the officials what it was like back in that year. I got 16 games the next year in the Pac-10 so I must have done something right.

Before I had any games in the PAC-10, I was at the PAC-10 camp thinking I knew everything about officiating on a two-person crew. At the camp the staff members were telling me conflicting things. One staff member told me to stand one place, somebody else told me to elsewhere. I opened my mouth and complained about the confusion how things were being taught, the staff member teaching was Carter Rankin on that floor. So he immediately ran to Ray DalPagetto the supervisor I was disagreeing with the way he wanted to have it done. So I was walking out in the hall and Ray stop me grab my shirt push me up against the wall and told me to stop being a Know-It-All or don't let the door hit me on the way out.

I sat down in the hall and tears were coming to my eyes and one of the other officials came by and saw me crying and asked what was wrong. I told her I was going to quit. I couldn't take the way I was being treated. What she said to me changed my life: she said I couldn't quit. "You're the future of women in officiating."

I'm so glad that I didn't quit and that I became an official in the PAC-10. That was when Ray gave me my one game for the season. I didn't know at the time how that one game was going to change the rest of my division one career. Either I reffed a spectacular one game or my attitude was a lot better. I didn't think about my emotions or anything, I never really did, I just knew I needed to have a better attitude and be open to learning new things. I was, I did, and it took me far.

My first game at Loyola University in the West Coast Conference was one day after Hank Gathers passed away in the same facility. Hank was a big star on the men's team, to the extent that the Loyola University's gym was referred to as the house that Hank built. It was my first time at Loyola, and the air was heavy. There simply wasn't a lot of cheering when normally you hear it immediately. That eerie emptiness is something I will never forget.

When I started traveling to officiate, we didn't have cell phones to keep us company on the road. There was hardly any per diem, so you basically spent your time in the car with your radio. My friend's husband worked for a Motorola company and put a phone in my car. I thought it was cool being able to drive and talk on the phone, until I got the first phone bill from my car phone. It was a big change for officials moving over to cell phones. At this time, you had to pay by the minute. I think Young officials today don't realize how difficult it was to communicate.

One time I was living in Redmond, Washington. I had a game at the University of Washington about 30 minutes from Redmond. Traffic was completely backed up I needed to cross a bridge to the University of Washington in order to get there on time. Just to communicate, I needed to take an exit before I was stuck on the bridge to find a payphone, (you remember those?) and tell my boss I was stuck in traffic. Lines of communication like payphones on the side of the road are so different than the convenience provided by cell phones now.

CHAPTER 15

Western Athletic Conference

One week before I went to camp in Texas to try out for the Western Athletic Conference, I sprained my ankle while stepping on first base in a softball game. I started crying, not from physical pain, but from the pain of knowing my tryout chances were in jeopardy. My teammates reacted to the physical pain, assuming I needed to get to the hospital. Meanwhile, I dwelled on the emotional pain, knowing my shot at making the conference was at stake. The tears kept flowing. I knew my softball career was coming to an end because I was trying to catch a fly ball and my eyes saw it in a different place and it hit me right in the forehead. I couldn't ignore this anymore.

I went to the camp and taped my ankle to the best of my ability at the camp. I was half-limping, half-running on the floor. Kaye Garms, the supervisor of the Western Athletic Conference, demanded I get off the floor. The authority in her voice startled me enough that I left for the training room to get the tape taken off my ankle immediately. I was crying, and in came Kaye to the training room. She said she intended to hire me anyway so it would be okay. She heard about my ability from other supervisors.

I never forgot how good her reassurance felt. She went out of her way to tell me that so I wouldn't work any more games at camp for my safety. I stayed and listened to all the lectures and was very excited to work in the Western Athletic Conference. I worried I wouldn't even work for them because of hurting my ankle, but some people always do the right thing Sometimes you just have to trust in people.

I owe great deal of my officiating career to Kaye. Because of this incident, I trust in people knowing that the right thing will happen.

Kaye Garms ~ Supervisor, Western Athletic Conference

As the coordinator of women's basketball officials for the Western Athletic Conference from 1990 to 2015 I attended division one women's basketball camps in order to observe, evaluate, and find good officials for our conference.

The first time I observed Dana Senders was at a camp at Texas Tech University in Lubbock. I noticed she had a remarkable feel for the game, had good communication skills with the players and coaches, and, most importantly kept the game, coaches, and players under control. She did her job quietly and efficiently, yet was not afraid to make the crucial call in a pressure situation.

Dana had sprained her ankle. However, I had observed her enough and hired her to work for the WAC. She continued to improve every season and I gained the utmost respect for Dana's ability as an official. She was soon chosen to officiate in our conference tournament and I recommended her to officiate in the NCAA division one tournament.

Dana had a passion for the game while officiating and maintained that passion as a division one coordinator of officials for the West Coast Conference and other division two conferences in the West Coast region. I feel fortunate to have had the opportunity to know and work with Dana as an official, friend, and coordinator.

My first WAC game was going to be at Utah with Elaine Elliott as the coach. I went to the airport, but the snow in Utah delayed my flight. Again, at that time there were no cell phones, but we all played over long distances, with pay phones. I called the University of Utah and spoke with Fern who was the athletic director at that time and she said they were hoping for me there and to keep her posted. This would be my first game at Utah so I felt stressed. My partner Lori needed to fly in from Los Angeles and she had similar problems getting to Utah.

Lori was connecting with me and the flight did take off I got there I landed and had to take a cab right to the college. I did not have time to check into a hotel first, I drove right to the University of Utah. The university had a huge stadium with the floor at the bottom of a lot of stairs. I didn't know there was an elevator or anything so I hurried down all the stairs to the locker room. Lori already made it and we were about 60 minutes away from game time.

Lori and I do a fast pregame and get dressed. Fern came in and thanked us both for getting there and we went out and worked the game. Back then we didn't have an observer, in the WAC, so we got the job done and got out of there. And yes, after that game we had to hike up all those stairs.

In those days, we worked back to back to back games, in the Western Athletic Conference. We had Thursday and Saturday. Our next game was in Provo, a 30-minute drive from Salt Lake City, so we stayed in a hotel that the university had a deal with. At that time, we never chose our hotels, the schools simply told us where to stay. Fortunately, they were usually nice hotels. We didn't have our game until Saturday so, with the snow outside, we stayed inside until Saturday. Being from LA, Lori was not familiar with snow. We allowed for extra-time and, being more familiar with snow, we chose me to drive down to Provo to BYU, to work the game.

CHAPTER 16
First Women

I was the first woman to officiate at Gonzaga University. The officials from Spokane had been working all their games Not only was I the first woman but I was also the first official west of the mountains to work at Gonzaga so, to say the least, they didn't have a locker room for a woman official. I had to dress in the storage room. It had a small shower and a small bathroom. I was getting dressed in this storage room and all of a sudden the door opened: it was the athletic director, who I later found out used this room to get dressed for the games. To say the least we were both a little embarrassed. I was in my sports bra we just kind of smiled at each other and he shut the door. The other locker room that my partner dressed in had a sofa, a nice shower and they even had an ice chest with sodas and beer in it.

My partner really didn't like that I was in charge. In this particular game, working the game and it happened to be Pepperdine at Gonzaga. It was a two-person crew with me as the lead official with my partner in the trail position. He called over and back on a girl with the ball. This violation occurs when the ball goes from the front court into the backcourt. She stopped right when he blew the whistle and was still in back court, so the violation never occurred. It was not a case of over and back so I went up to my partner and said to call inadvertent whistle and give them back the ball out of bounds. He looked me square in the eyes, crossed his arms, and told me if I didn't like the call, I could make the change myself.

So, I did. I ran over to both coaches to explain the situation and reverse the call. The Pepperdine coach told me he wasn't happy when an official change a call against me, but that was the right thing to do.

The Spokane official didn't like me and probably never forgave me for that call change. He was not brought back to the conference the next year and I was in the conference for many years to come, so I didn't need to worry about him. Doing the right thing is more important than hurt feelings, even if it involves an uncomfortable change. Everyone could see that the player never entered the front court. I don't believe in changing your partner's call as a habit, but if a wrong call is clear to everyone in the gym, then you have to make the right decision.

Mark Trakh ~ (Pepperdine University coach) New Mexico State coach, and now University of Southern California).

I have the utmost respect for Dana Senders.

When I communicated with her regarding our WCC Officials, she was always fair and impartial. There were many times that she strongly supported her officials in calls that were made during the games. But Dana did not blindly support her officials. There were times when she agreed with us on calls and took appropriate action.

If Dana told me a call was correct, I did not question her judgement and accepted that judgement. And I respected her judgement on those times she agreed with me. This led to a relationship that was built on mutual respect and trust. In short, I trusted Dana to do the right thing for all parties involved. She was a great coordinator of officials in my humble opinion.

CHAPTER 17

2ⁿᵈ Year

I was going to the PAC-10 camp, my second year in the conference at Washington State University. Ray the supervisor rented a big white Cadillac. Eight Women would drive over to Pullman from Spokane with five women in the back and the rest in front with Ray. We were so crammed into that car that we really got to know each other. Kathleen McGlynn, Peggy Franz-Gettis were all in the back seat of this big old Cadillac with me, and we all became good friends at that moment because we were so tight. Since there were so few of us I knew we needed to stick together to help women in officiating.

Once we got to Pullman, it was a hundred degrees without air conditioning in the dorms or the gym, so the eight women were on one floor of the dorms and the twenty-two men were down in the other floor. Peggy was ill, so we had to cover her games for her. It was so hot there that it was impossible to stay hydrated, but we got through it. I was in the printing business, so I printed special T-shirts that said, "we survived the PAC-10 camp in Pullman, Washington in 1990". I have since lost my shirt, but I asked my friend Tom Dubus if he still had his shirt, and he did and gave it to me. So I get to wear that shirt again from 27 years ago when I printed it. I never knew how much it would mean to me.

The camp was so hot after working 3 games in one day, I headed right to the shower when one of the referees came in and told me I needed to get out because we were having a meeting downstairs. So I got dressed and went downstairs and found a surprise party for my 33rd birthday waiting for me. Ray had a big sheet cake, flowers, and a PAC 10 watch. I remember that party as the start of my first full year in the PAC-10. This was also my first division one season after I was diagnosed with MS. So I would say that this was the biggest change in my whole life. I just had my 60th birthday and Tom Dubus was at my party 27 years after my 33rd.

CHAPTER 18
MS Diagnosis

How my diagnosis was discovered. In the spring of 1990 I woke up with blurriness in my eyes for the third day in a row. Made the decision I needed to go to the doctor. After a few tests, my regular eye doctor made me very nervous, he called another doctor to look at my eyes. He said I needed an optic neurologist as soon as possible. He made the appointment, and I drove to Seattle to see him.

After he checked my eyes he told me I had optic neuritis so at 33 I got my first does of steroids, not knowing at that time I would have a few dozen more in my life time. The neurologist handed me a pamphlet about optic neuritis about "75% of women with optic neuritis have multiple sclerosis."

Well, I would just need to be in the 25% and Beat It. Needless to say, that did not happen.

I didn't want to tell anybody I had MS, and, at first, I could pull it off. Numbness grew in my left leg. My leg grew weaker and weaker, impacting my running starting in 1994. I refereed for four years after I was diagnosed in 1990. I knew my referee career was coming to a close. At that time in 1990 there was not hardly any medication for MS. All I knew about it was I didn't want it and was going to fight it and ignore it as long as I could. I fought it as best I could along the road acted like I wasn't getting sick and just tried to stay strong.

When I was supervisor they came up with the new option for people with MS. they put a balloon into your carotid that was supposed to open it up which was to help people with MS. If I had a blockage they did an ultrasound of my neck first and that was done in Washington. The procedures were only done in Tucson AZ... Flight Arizona to get this done and come up with the money they found a blockage it was worth a try $8,000 but I was willing to try anything. Insurance didn't cover it. After I worked with the insurance company, I filled out all the forms and duplicated it and went through everything actually got the insurance to pay me back the $8,000. It didn't help me any but I'm glad that I tried it. Fly down to Arizona to try the procedure because they didn't do it in Washington but it was worth the effort. My sister lives in Tucson so I got to see her.

Before all of that I had a game at Oregon State. I drove from Seattle down to Portland where I met with my partner Bob Olson the weather in Oregon that really turn to ice and Bob and his car phone so we did call Oregon State let them know we were coming. We called Ray. He said he could get an alternate there that lives close to the school in case we didn't make.

The game was at 7 we pulled into the parking lot at 6:30. Bob said let's go in the front door so everyone knows we're here so I almost killed myself going in the front door at the gym slipping on the iced over steps, but everyone was happy to see us. We headed to the locker room to change. The alternate was there, happy that we had arrived. Besides Utah, this is the only time that I almost missed a game because of weather. My MS was in my mind but I would not let it affect my officiating.

CHAPTER 19

Official and Coaches Thoughts

Marcy was spectacular at all the clinics. Marcy became a very good friend of mine even though we don't see each other to often. She came to a few of my camps, we always got to have lunch together while she was there, and she attended my retirement from my camps as well as my 50th and my 60th birthday party I can't tell you what a great friend she has become and tell where my life would be without her. I love her dearly.

As an official, I met a gentleman named Tom Dubus, Tom and I have became very good friends. At Pac 10 meeting at the NCAA Clinic, Carter Rankin was now in charge of the pac-10 officials. Tom kept asking questions going longer and longer. I sent a note back to Tom stop asking questions the best part of all this was Tom kept that note for all the years. He gave it back to me at my retirement party almost 25 years later, it truly made me smile and my heart warm that he would have kept this note all that time in his wallet. What an awesome note of affection. Tom worked at most of my camps and at several PAC-10 and WCC games when I was officiating.

Tom Dubus

The first memory of Dana that I have is at a PAC-10 camp for prospective new officials. I was a counselor and could see immediately the fire and passion she had for the game. I was blessed to work with and for her for a great many years. I especially enjoyed working at her summer camps. They were long days, but a lot of fun. It has been an inspiration to see the devotion she has had for the advancement of Women's Basketball and to see all of the officials she mentored and brought into division one basketball.

One of my fondest memories was a year when I had a day off between two Pac-10 games and she asked me to come to Santa Clara to work in the WCC Tournament on my day off. I injured my leg in the first PAC-10 game and was limping badly when I arrived in Santa Clara. I informed her of the injury and she said, "Let's see how you feel in the morning." She said she would have an alternate ready, if I couldn't go. I did not sleep a wink that night. I spent it icing and praying. I felt some better in the morning and when I got to the arena, the trainer spent a lot of time prepping and wrapping it properly. Dana left it up to me as to whether or not I wanted to work. I said I'd try and I was blessed to get through the game fine and do a game the next day as well.

I will always be grateful and indebted to Dana for letting me make the decision as to when I wanted to stop working division one basketball. That was not always the case with other conferences. I will always feel blessed to count her among my dearest friends!

One time I was at Pauley Pavilion at UCLA. They were playing University of California under Coach Foster on Super Bowl Sunday. My partner and I let them play without penalizing too harshly because the game was not close. We were just trying to let the game finish, not have anyone get hurt there was a play with the post player from UCLA going to the basket with a few people on her arm but she put the ball up in. So I didn't call any foul. The game continued on I passed by Coach Kathy from UCLA and she asked if I had a Super Bowl party to get to. I smiled at her. "Yes, I do."

I didn't actually have a party to go to, I just thought it was funny, she smiled and the game went on. That same year I was working a Tournament game at the University of Portland I ran into the coach from Eastern Washington in the hall who was in the loser's bracket of the tournament and I had just seen him at a tournament at Washington State. He asked why I was on all of his games. I thought to myself that if he wasn't in the loser's bracket, I wouldn't have him.

I went out to do the game with a weaker official when I found myself having to carry the game. In those days, you had to get three technicals to be ejected. The coach at Eastern Washington had his first technical when he yelled at my partner. His second technical was yelling at me. When I went over to him and asked him do you want to stay in the game, he told me he'd just as soon not be there with me officiating. I gave him his third technical and ejected him from the game.

In my 20 years on the court, I never ejected another coach, even when it only took two technicals to be ejected. The funny thing about that particular ejection was his assistant coach stepped up to beat Portland. They were behind when the coach had to leave.

At the University of Portland, I had to get dressed in the room where they kept the extra chairs. This particular outing, I accidentally left my wet sweaty underwear not knowing that I left anything there. The senior women's administrator from Portland found them, washed them, and had them for me the next game that I worked at University of Portland. This kindness was a trait I found in all of the University of Portland staff, and I believe that's why Jim Sollars and Kelly Graves, the assistant coach at the time, were always in my corner.

Kelly Graves, Women's Basketball Coach, University of Oregon

"It's not often you hear a coach praise an official but I thoroughly enjoyed working with Dana over the years. She would set me straight when I was a young brash coach but did so with caring and a sense of humor. Dana was an excellent official with

the ability to be a great communicator with coaches and I very much appreciated her style. As a supervisor of officials, did a great job of preparing and mentoring a young group of referees. Our game is better because she was a part."

Pages from a notebook: UW women are in style

n the 1990s, when Northwest women want to see the latest fashion statements, they go to University of Washington women's games and check out what coach Chris Gobrecht and assistants Willette White and Kathy Anderson are wearing.

Very spiffy.

■ It's not often you hear people saying nice things about basketball officials, and it's even more rare to hear compliments about officials at women's games.

That made it all the more significant on Sunday to hear people remarking about the job Dana Senders did in the Washington-Oregon State game Friday.

CHAPTER 20
Looking for Partner Help

I was working a Western Athletic Conference tournament game at Utah. There were two of us on the game at this time when I had a ball coming my way going out of bounds. As I called the direction of the out-of-bounds, I saw a player kick another player, so I issued a technical, and went over to the bench. I barely turned around before I saw a girl take a swing at another girl, so I ejected the player that took the swing. The coach from the bench yelled at me and said the swing was an example of retaliation and that I missed the first hit. I could only eject the second player because I did not see the first swing. I asked my partner if he saw something different and he didn't.

This turned out to be interesting because there was less than two minutes to go in the game and the team that had the player ejected lost. I was in the stands watching my fellow officials on the next game when the angered coach started yelling again. I told him I could only call what I saw. We saw the tape to verify what happened everyone could see the player I ejected was the only player to take a swing. I didn't get the support I needed from my partner or our alternate in defending my call. This a true example of where 3 officials would have helped.

Another experience I had I was working my second year in the NCAA Tournament, and had to change planes in Denver through the old Denver Airport. The airport was sort of H-shaped, so you'd start on one end of the airport, go to a different elbow of the airport, then head to another, so, of course, I was running late. It was a tight fit for me to get to the other flight running through the airport with one bag over each shoulder. I'm running to catch this flight. I come around the corner, but see no people waiting to get on the plane. I only see one airline person standing by the gate.

"Are you Senders?"

"Yes."

"We've been holding the plane for you."

My face shouted: SHOCK. I entered the plane and was told to take a seat with everybody on the plane already seated and staring at me. I sat down as quick as I could, wiped the sweat from my brow, and felt so fortunate to have a plane wait for me. I made it to my game in Lubbock Texas, with my friend Larry Shepherd.

At this time, the observer at each game would call the National coordinator about how the officials did for advancement in the tournament. I was in my hotel room after the game and realize that the observer was in the room next door and I so desperately wanted to hear her review of the game. So I had heard or seeing ways you could listen through walls with a glass so the funny thing was I put a glass up to the wall to see if I could listen to see if I would be advancing in the tournament. I really couldn't hear I did hear a few things that were nice that my Observer was saying to the national coordinator. I think this is particularly funny because in this year we were telephoned after we got home if we would advance in the tournament. Both Larry and I got a call to advance.

Larry Shepherd

My only recollection of that time was that "Women's Basketball" referred to the players, not the officials. The NCAA had recently taken over the Women's Basketball Play-offs and there were very few female officials around the country, and especially on the West Coast. Leagues were looking for women who could officiate at the Division I level, but there were very few available and most who tried were not ready for that level of participation. Dana was one of the first that I saw who had the attitude, confidence, and ability to make it to the top level of competition, although we needed to work on the attitude part of the equation. She was able to do that over the next few years and I often reflect back on our game together in Lubbock and how well you worked at the NCAA Play-Off level."

Early that same year I had a game at Central Washington University during Christmas break, about a two-hour drive from Seattle. I realized I forgot my striped shirt back at home when I packed for the game. I asked for somebody with a key to the intramural office because I thought there might be an official's shirt in there, but, being Christmas break, no one had a key available. I asked a coach if there was a sporting goods store nearby, but he told me one of her players was married to a high school referee who would bring a shirt for me to wear. I did have a gray T-shirt in my bag that I could wear probably just as well as my officiating shirt. I wasn't really nervous because I knew that would work for me I took him up on the players husband, hoping that I wouldn't have to wear the T-shirt. He showed up with his shirt: a double extra-large with the high school insignia sewn onto the shirt. Since I didn't have a choice, I put the shirt on. Being 5'4" and about 134 pounds, the shirt was quite large for me, coming all the way down to my knees. But at least it was a referee shirt! I did my best to tuck in all of the shirt into my pants and I rolled the sleeves up a little bit to referee with that shirt. I didn't have time to wash the shirt after the game, but he was okay with washing it himself. I never forget about that game because I have never forgotten a shirt since; I remembered to pack two shirts for every game after that.

CHAPTER 21

Carried our Bag when Traveling

Many officials likely don't remember when we didn't have little roller bags. All of our officiating gear went in one bag that we carried over our shoulder. In those days, that was it.

I first saw a roller bag while working alongside Becky Marshall. It was a WAC tournament game and I thought the roller bag was silly. She should be carrying it on the shoulder like the rest of us! It turns out, she had it right. We were wrong. I probably would have saved one of my shoulders if I had a roller bag while officiating over the years! Both my shoulders have torn rotator cuffs, and, although I'm not sure actually what caused all the tears in my shoulders actually from I think years of softball, an awkward fall straight onto my arm, and years of officiating with a heavy bag on my shoulders all have a little bit to do with the injuries to me. Not looking more into repairing the tears sooner was a mistake I made.

32 States Sports Took Me

CHAPTER 22

After Diagnosis Tell Your Boss

After I had been diagnosed with MS, I was driving to Western Washington University in Bellingham, Washington for to a division two game. My partner, Malcolm Boyle, asked if it was true that I had MS. I was taken aback. I hadn't told anyone, so I was surprised he knew that. I told him I'd rather not talk about it and he was quiet for a minute. We changed the subject and went on to do a great game, he never brought MS up again and no partner ever asked that question, after that day, and I never brought it up because I didn't want to talk about it too anyone!

My next to last year I needed to fly to Washington State for a game, but one of my legs wasn't working very well, the MS had started to really affect my body.

I asked my roommate to drive me over to Pullman, it would be the death of me trying to fly. I made it through that game, but suddenly I didn't think I could officiate a game for the Western Athletic Conference. I told Kaye Garms over the phone that it was too snowy to get to the game. It was not true, but, in retrospect, I can say it's better to tell your supervisor when you are having a hard time. I just had a hard time admitting it to myself. She was angry with me because finding a fill-in for a game was challenging. She called me days later, pissed off so at that point, so I decided I needed to tell her about my MS. I never told any of my supervisors at this point, she was the first. She was mad at me because I didn't tell the truth, but she understood now. She told me I needed to be honest and tell her if I could keep working. I said I was feeling much better at this time and didn't think there would be a problem. For the rest of the season, I did not have any exacerbation the rest of the season, in fact, that is the year that I went to the elite 8 in Arkansas, for the NCAA tournament. Over the course of the next season, my left leg began to grow weaker. I knew this would be my last season. This upset me, but I wanted to do as much as I could do for myself as a sendoff. That's why I chose to go to the NAIA national tournament in Tennessee instead of working the NCAA.

One of my first years in the WAC, I officiated a game at San Diego state with a male partner. Our locker room set up was unusual, again it was tough for my partners because these gyms were not set up with gendered shower facilities, so after the game, I let him take a shower first and I moved behind a row of lockers. After he finished showering, he moved over to the restroom area where I could not see him and I went around to the shower. There were no shower partitions and, from around the corner, he walked into the open space where he could see me showering. He began talking casually, but I asked him to leave, I wanted privacy while I showered. He became defensive, insisting he was only talking to me, but I told him he had no right to stand and talk to me while causing me discomfort. He finally went back over to the lockers. I finished showering and went to the bathroom to get dressed.

After I left the gym I called my assigner Kaye Garms and told her my experience. The situation wasn't uncommon, and I was only told I would never have to work with him again. This was not really the answer that I wanted to hear but it was sufficient. Three-person crews were still off in the future, so now I'm not sure exactly how such an event would be handled, but I hope all officials respect each other so they don't put themselves in the same situation. All woman officials need to see the road worked before them, because I know this situation felt really uncomfortable to me and I would never want it to happen again.

Kristi Brodin ~ Former Coach and AD, Northwest College NAIA

I think that most women's b-ball games I attend I think of Dana! You are the standard by which I measure the officials I watch... and usually they fall short!! You were not only a GREAT official in the technical sense (and did you every make a bad call?? :-)) but you were also a great professional and teacher to the younger ones. And when I coached I very much appreciated the way you could keep things professional, but at the same time have fun and relate to both players and coaches appropriately! Thanks for all you have done for the game!!"

That same year I officiated back-to-back games at San Diego State, and I worked my game Thursday. My partner made a call against a San Diego State player shooting at the three-point line with not too much time left—only about a minute. The call was iffy from my perspective. The game moves down to the other end where I am the lead, and we have the same type of call. I don't blow my whistle because it wasn't a legit call. So the visitor won the game. On the news that night, there's a big story about the call my partner made: a foul with no contact.

So what can I do but go back to the gym on my Saturday game with a different partner. Beth Burns, the coach at San Diego State, asked me a question.

"Would you have made that call?"

I said, "Beth, you know I can't answer that."

"Well that's the answer I'm looking for."

I was never asked that question again. I feel that coaches respected me enough to think my calls were unquestionable. During back-to-back games at the Western Athletic Conference, I would see coaches multiple times. I felt respected, and hoped they were happy to see me come on the floor.

During another game at San Diego state, I was running down the sidelines to get ahead of the play and I tripped ass over tea kettle on Beth Burns's feet. She started laughing and offered her hand to pick me up. I was more embarrassed than anything so I said no thank you and got up by myself. Really the only problem was my partner saw me on the floor and didn't stop the game and when I looked at him he was sort of chuckling. I wasn't hurt the game went on but I still have that look of amazement on my face that coach Beth was actually laughing when I ended up on the floor.

One weekend right before a game at Gonzaga, I forgot to pack my pants. I called my partner, Bob Olson, who was driving from Portland to hurry and pick me up. I needed to go to the store to buy elastic waist pants for our game at Gonzaga. Back then, we still did not have lycra under game pants, so I didn't have to worry about being able to put the pants over undergarments at least so I found some at Sears. We went to the game, Portland at Gonzaga, and +I was familiar with the coaches of both teams. Bob thought it would be funny to tell the Portland coach about my new stretchy pants. So during one call, I went over to coach Jim Sollars, thinking it was funny, and he said I must have made that call because my new pants were too tight. We both had a chuckle and then back to the game we went.

Jim Sollars ~ Coach, University of Portland, Division One (Retired)

The best part of working with you besides the friendship we developed through the years was your willingness to listen to coaches' complaints, no matter how petty. You understood that sometimes we just had to vent and didn't really expect you to do anything about it. Not many people can do that!

On I went. To my next assignment because I needed to fly down to Portland for a game at Oregon and had my roommate fly down a box with my regular pair of pants so I have them for my game, so I got a big lesson to start having duplicates of everything and making sure when I pack to have a list.

CHAPTER 23

Canada Woman Officials

Jake Steinbrener, an official who attended my camp, asked me to speak at one his local meetings in Alberta. I flew to Canada to give a little talk for a group that had about 8 women out of a group of 50. During my talk, they started asking questions about women officiating in the states. My speech stopped there and out came the questions about officiating in the states.

After I was done in the meeting room I met two wonderful women officials that wanted to know more. I offered to let them come to my camp on scholarship. If they could simply get there, I assured them they would not have to pay for camp. They came to my camp in Portland and did an awesome job, so I offered another free camp in Los Angeles to Pepperdine. They made it over there to Pepperdine and had a great time, so I offered them a job working division two at a small college in Washington. Again, they did a great job, so I offered Karen Lasuik a spot in the West Coast Conference Division 1 if she could find a way to get a green card so I helped. She went to a lawyer and figured out a way to get a green card, although it would cost quite a bit of money. That's what she did and she started working division one.

Eventually, she did so well that she ended up working the WCC conference tournament. After some hard work, I am so proud to say she took a little bit of me with her to the 2016 Olympics to officiate women's basketball.

Karen Lasuik

I met Dana in 1998 when she was invited to our officiating seminar as a guest speaker in my home town of Edmonton, Alberta. There were about 8 women officials in a sea of men at this seminar, and I remember Dana saying something along the lines of, "Is this all the women officials you have in this city?" During her talk, she helped to promote the women in the group, telling us we can be successful as a female in a male dominated avocation, and if we wanted to come work in the US, we would be given that opportunity. Being in a male dominated "boys club" in our local officiating associations, this tweaked the interest in a few of us. So off we went to Dana's West Coast Officials Camp in Portland. What an eye opener! After this camp, Dana told the few of us,

"You need to come to my other camp this summer and meet Bill Crowley, a Canadian Official who could help the 3 of us make it to the top ranks of officiating in Canada. I took advantage of this and low and behold, the next season, I was invited to try out for my International Officiating License!

I will never forget the first camp I went to, I called a foul and bird-dogged (pointed at the player who fouled). Dana came roaring over and pretty much said, "What the hell was that you just did?" I told her it was a "bird-dog" and that's what we do in Canada. She responded with, "Well you're not in Canada anymore—lose it!" So to ensure I would not be tempted on my next foul call, when I blew my whistle, I put my hand in my pocket so I could not point!

Dana would always say, "I can only open the door - it's up to you to walk through". Well when she provided me with the opportunity to work for her, I JUMPED through that door!"

After one of my 25 camps still officiating I visited Montana only once, in the dark. During work I got a phone call to referee at Montana in Missoula, in early November to work the WNIT a pre-season national tournament. I got off work, packed my clothes, and went right down to the airport, straight to Montana.

There was some trouble picking up my tickets. The attendant checked for my last name Senders, but had no luck. After a bit of trial and error, we thought maybe my ticket would be under a similar sounding last name. It wasn't Cinders. We went down the list of tickets alphabetically and found my name under Dana Fenders. My flight was about to leave, so I grabbed my ticket, boarded the flight, and I was off to Montana.

I arrived in the dark with my partner nowhere in sight. We had a backup plan for a no-show, but, until then, I worked the pregame with a local high school official. With a high school official was challenging he'd never worked a college game so I did the best I could to get him ready in case my partner did not show. My partner finally showed up, a bit closer to the game time than I would have liked, we ran through a fast pre-game, and then started the game.

I found out quickly during that one visit how Montana crowds worked: they booed everything we called against Missoula and shouted if they perceived any missed calls. I finished our game, went to my hotel, and then flew off on an early morning flight. I have never seen Montana in the daylight.

The Big Sky Conference commissioner at that time would never hire me to Big Sky, especially with that being my one and only trip to the Big Sky. In all honesty, with the way the Missoula crowd treated officials, it would be a tough place to go to.

CHAPTER 24
Be Totally Honest

I was already in the Pac 10, Western Athletic, and the West Coast Conferences, so I decided to try out for another conference: the Big West Conference. I roomed at the Big West camp with Lisa Ulmer and Carla Fujimoto. Palm Springs was so hot my shoes stuck to the pavement.

My one and only experience in Palm Springs for basketball was getting hired and fired in the same week. I tried to save a nickel, and it came back to me in a bad way.

My mother, a travel agent at the time, got me a ticket to Palm Springs. I had free ticket from Alaska airlines, and I thought nothing of my mom writing a receipt for what the cost would have been. I flew over, got the ticket receipt, and turned it into the Big West Conference supervisor, I had no intention of causing trouble. But, to Andrea, the situation looked like I lied to her and tried to use conference money for the trip. So the same week I was hired for the Big West Conference, I was fired over a free flight. I never forgave Andrea for that, but still, when she sees me, she always hugs me. I don't think she even remembers. I almost had the Big West on my résumé, but it was not meant to be, over me not thinking. Lesson learned.

That was my first time getting fired from a conference, but I learned a lot. I didn't even think of not telling the full truth to any official after that. You shouldn't try to save a nickel when it might end up costing you dimes!

There was a role reversal at one of my camps in Portland, later on. An official worked very hard so I offered him a contract for the WCC. One game later, he made terrible calls all game, so I pulled him aside and told him it just wasn't the right year to hire him. I think he was devastated, but he worked that much harder his next season and I eventually did hire him. It made him a better official and made me a better supervisor knowing to watch somebody a bit more closely, so in a sense, I understand where Andrea was coming from. But I also believe in giving hard workers second chances. Also waiting that year helped his career because he later made it to the NCAA tournament.

CHAPTER 25

Camps

The biggest change in officiating since I began was moving from two officials to three officials. Working with two officials is how I refereed my whole career until my last year on the floor. It was confusing for the staff of the conference to teach us how to work with three officials. It felt like the third official was just in the way. But having three officials meant careers could last longer and the courts could be covered much better. I didn't think we needed a third and at first, nobody knew where to look or where to stand. That would be the biggest thing. One other change was the size of the ball changing from men's basketball to a smaller ball. I wished the ball size could have been smaller when I played, I liked this change. It's a huge advantage for the players.

To this day I'm not sure if it was right or not that I had to end my officiating career. Everything went okay through the 17 years and 25 camps. I never look back because I was still doing everything I wanted to as a supervisor, and I handled everything in my scooter, during those last 10 years of camps when I could not walk. The weirdest thing is I never felt sick until the last year supervising, the end of my thirty-fifth year involved in women's basketball officials. I still didn't feel sick but I did retire at my retirement party, but the end of my camps was the end of me supervising.

The party was put together by Carla. It was one of the best days of my life. I had a few good days in my life, but this one was a surprise that I didn't know was going to happen at a classroom at the University of Washington was above the gym over the facilities the only thing for me to get to the room was the elevator. To keep it a secret, Carla had someone stand by the elevator. If I was coming up, they were to let her know. She was working on an awesome book with "Danaisms". These Danaisms are phrases I would tell everybody frequently and they became ingrained in their minds and tied to who I am and how I worked.

In all my years, I have never been surprised before, but they got me. I was about to close the camp out for that day just to give a little talk. Marla Denham, who was the supervisor of the Big Sky Conference, interrupted me, saying she had something to say. So she stood up in front of the class and started talking about me. Then it was Marcy's turn and at the end they handed me a beautiful award with a whistle attached to it thanking me for all my years of service to women's basketball and officiating in the West Coast Conference. This was such a surprise to me and I can't even imagine a better ending for officiating service. I got hugs from everybody and a great picture with the whole group. I hated being in pictures, specifically in my scooter. Something was weird when I was getting the camp staff together knowing a smaller camp because I was no longer a division one supervisor so I told them that I didn't need as many staff this year. I thought it was strange when they all insisted on coming. However, I didn't put it all together until that surprise party, so I had a lot more staff then I needed for 65 campers.

CHAPTER 26

Meeting the National Coordinator

In 1991, I met Marcy Weston, the national coordinator of woman's referees for the whole country. I was at the official's clinic in San Francisco in the elevator going up to my room. She was in the elevator with me. I put out my hand to shake hers.

"My name is Dana Senders."

She said, "I know who you are."

This came over me like a warm blanket. The boss of everybody recognized who I was. That was the first year I was assigned to work the first round in the NCAA national tournament.

Interview with Marcy Weston

I saw Dana work, when her name was recommended, I put her on to send her to the next game in the tournament. I think the first year she worked upward to working the first and second round of the championship. I was always proud to see her working on the floor.

I ended up meeting her on the elevator. I said, "Hi Dana!" She knew me because we did regional clinics, and she was surprised I remembered her name and that was how it started.

I saw her work more ahead to being in the late 90's when the MS started kicking in. She had to take herself out of refereeing, her running had slightly declined. At the time I was doing everything by myself, so I asked if I could have an assistant. They said yes, tell us who you want. I picked Dana from the West Coast and another woman from the East side of the country.

Later she asked me to come out and speak at a couple of officiating camps out in Washington and Oregon, I flew out and spent some time speaking at her camp and working with her. She was an excellent teacher, and an excellent coach on how to officiate, so I didn't need to tell her anything. I tried to get out there once a year to let people know I was interested in them. So I went out and spent four or five days a couple of times. I then went out for her fiftieth birthday, she was still working camps at the time. I flew out to Washington to kind of surprise her.

She is small in stature, she's not very tall, but she was a dynamo on the court, a take-charge kind of person. She goes back to when there were two, not three, officials. She took charge appropriately. A referee needs a little more experience and a little more take charge of a person. She was very strong on the court, not overbearing, but strong, confident, and self-assured. Everybody remembers her because she's not very tall, but she ran very, very well. I want her to think of all of the good things she were able to do, but know that even though you can't do everything you used to do, you can still have the same impact.

She ran camps and clinics. She would scooter around to the different places and the gym, use her van to get from one side to the other. She never let her physical ineptness take her confidence and drive. She just fought through it and fought through it and fought through it. She did so much work for officials that both young and even veteran officials would go to Dana for assurance. "Take a look at the game and help me get better." She continues to be a dynamo even now that she can't get around very much, she has key people who will call her and let her know what her work meant to them.   I saw Karen work a game during the last Olympics. Dana made a big difference in her life.

She made a big impact on a lot of people. I said, "Dana you need to write a book." There are a lot of people who would want to hear your thoughts. It's a lot different officiating today than it was in the 70's and 80's, and I started in the 60's, so to hear that from Dana would make a big difference to a lot of people.

One story I can remember starts with Dana calling all of her officials in. She's a little person, and she's got all these men and women standing around her, hovering over her. She's a speaker in a huge amphitheater, intently listening. She had so many different experiences that she could share with them. There is the technical side, but also how to deal with people. What do you do when there is a hot-headed athlete? You can imagine her with all these six-foot-high women and you got this feisty five-foot-tall woman who was probably tougher than all of them.

When she would bring them in, they would sit cross legged or stand around her and she would sit in her chair and she was the center of their focus. The way she captured the last session, she would pick out a person to share an individual story, and they would need to be ready. She could command the room as an officiating teacher or "clinician". Almost everybody was younger than her, but she had a few older than her who came to her camps striving to get better in their career and they came in over the summer.

Her drive is unbelievable. There are people who would have folded in half, turned it off, and said I'm stepping away. Her fortitude, perseverance, and love of the game of basketball and of the people who manage the game kept her going. She loves being a teacher. She loves being an official's coach. She would never slow down, she would get in her van, go to the hotel, get up in the morning. I say that in a good way because she wasn't going to let everything take her down. She kept her eye on your prize, keep her focus, and her goal was to make officials better. That was all she thought of. It kept her from self-pity. It kept her from feeling sorry for herself. It kept her focused on the things she could do, not the things she could not do. She could do pretty much everything except run and walk before.

She still had her mind, her upper body, her brain, her personality. She's feeling those kind of ebb away with th the physical part of it. I'm starting to forget things a little bit. I said "Dana, you forgot things, you're forty. We all forget things." I'm sure it's real. It's a shitty situation. If you've got two days to live when you're forty, you think "shoulda, coulda, woulda." You've got this right now. This is how you get everything and bring it all together and show how you were a contributor and made basketball a better game. We all walk in a gym, I watch kids today who are at my school, some of them drop their head and say we can't stand them. Or they smile because they think there are fair officials. Some people get the job done, some people don't get the job done. Dana always go the job done. I call her every week to ten days to make sure she's staying on her book mission.

CHAPTER 27

Elite 8 Hardest Year of My Life. Broke My Foot

I met Leon Barmore the coach from LA Tech and got to talk him down.

It was the USC/LA Tech regional final in Fayetteville, Arkansas. Tina Thompson from USC was falling out of bounds with the ball calling for a timeout. At that time the rules allowed for a player to call a time out when you have control of the ball when falling out of bounds. I granted it to her and Leon Barmore yelled at me from the sidelines. I went over and said if you stop yelling I'll talk to you. I could picture a lightbulb switching on over his head. He said oh I am yelling, but what did you call? I explained that Tina had control of the ball, and that the ball was legal at that time when Tina called for a timeout. He had already thrown his jacket off earlier in the game.

During the Elite 8 game at USC sidelines a ball went out of bounds right in front of Cheryl Miller, the USC coach. It was on table-side and we were in Cadillac position, meaning the trail is on the left hand side of the court, so I was a long way from the ball. The ball came from the other side of the floor near the baseline, far from me. I gave the ball to LA Tech. Cheryl put her arm around me and said you didn't see the ball hit off LA Tech? I mentioned that if there been three officials, we could have caught that, but, with only two, I could only trust what I saw. And on we went. At that time I didn't know that three-person crews were right around the corner. I later saw Coach Cheryl and her team inside the very small Fayetteville airport. She asked me why I wasn't in the PAC-10. I said I really was, but I didn't make the assignments of our games. She said J didn't see you during the season. She said I'm going to ask for you on more games, but she left USC at the end of the year so I never saw her again. You really aren't supposed to talk to the coach after the game, but the Fayetteville Airport waiting room didn't offer a way around seeing her and her team. I ended up feeling great about it, at least until the plane was late leaving and I missed my connection in Dallas to get home.

1990, when I was diagnosed with MS, going to 1995 were the five hardest years of my life. After being diagnosed with MS I knew I had to do some things that I would probably not be able to do later in life. So I went rock climbing. I felt comfortable climbing rocks, but I had some difficulties and decided it was too scary to try again. I went white water rafting, which was an adrenaline rush, but I needed my feet to hold on and my legs were growing weak, so I decided not to do that again. For my officiating career, I worked my way up through the NCAA tournament and, after the fourth year, went to the Elite 8. I thought I could still ref, so I started a fifth year. I was offered to do the tournament for the NAIA national tournament In Tennessee, this was the 3rd year I had been invited. Since I was doing things I knew I wouldn't be able to do soon, I decided to accept the NAIA invitation because I thought 1995 would be my last year officiating. The tournament ran two-person crews which I was most familiar with, but they had all officials work 2 games a day. Each game I taped my ankle from my 1975 surgery though 20 years ago my ankle was only in need of support at the end of the season.

I had worked over 50 games that season. So on my 3rd game in two days with a minute and a half to go, I felt as though a knife stabbed through the bottom of my foot. These tournament games all have a stand-by official or alternate who sits at the table, but I didn't have alternates on regular season games, so I didn't even think about it. I had to limp my way through. As the game ended, I limped my way down. The stairs to the locker room. 8 people followed me. The doctor came in and told me I would need my ankle x-rayed. The doctor's office was right down the street. One of the female officials helped me change and gave me crutches that helped me get to the doctor's car, and we went to the off to his office.

The x-ray showed I completely broke a bone in my foot. The doctor gave me a walking boot and returned to the tournament. I was scheduled for the finals, but I couldn't work anymore. The head of the officials asked if I wanted to either stay or go home. I chose to go home.

Later at the small Fayetteville airport, a guy came up to me and asked if that was me in the paper? He handed me a paper showing me, the referee who broke her foot in the tournament. I said wow this is what they think of even the officials in this tournament. In Dallas, I rolled up to the counter in a wheelchair and the gal checking me in said they reserved three seats for me to lie down. How did they hear about me? Please, please tell me what happened? This made my last game as an official very important in the game of women's basketball.

Later I found out from my friend Marcy that if I had a good tournament I could have gone to the Final Four. I always say, "Woulda, coulda, shoulda." While that was the end of my refereeing career on the floor, really my referee life was simply changing. Marcy was the national coordinator the next year and she asked me to be her assistant.

So I flew home knowing that I would have refereed the finals if not for my broken foot. That ended my career as a basketball official. I was essentially the number one official out of the Northwest, as well as the number one woman. But my multiple sclerosis went with my officiating career. But I realized I had more to accomplish, so becoming the boss seemed like the next step along with camps. I became the supervisor of the West Coast Conference, the supervisor of division two in the Great Northwest conference, and division three in the North-West Conference. The commissioner from division two was very difficult to work with and it was a challenge to keep my officials strong every game possible. I could not quit that job, even though he made my work very difficult, I couldn't let my coaches or officials down. Even though it was so emotionally difficult I just kept my head down and worked like I always did. One thing that had not happened yet was professional women's basketball. A little pro league for women was the ABL, American basketball league for women to get paid to play and they hired me to observe the officials. I was walking with a cane but it kept me in the game right after I retired so as an official. Soon I would be in a scooter. Then the WNBA started the ABL ended and they did not need me to observe.

I did not walk anymore, so I was the supervisor in a scooter. I met as many officials as I could. I would go to multiple games from schools in all locations. I have to really commend all of the officials of the West Coast Conference because if they were willing to stay and work small College for me that would be great, it would often be for a small amount of money. I think they did it just out of respect for me.

I loved officiating so much to be the best I could be and put considerable effort into being that same effort as supervisor. I needed to take elevators to the game site, had my scooter go up and down to get on the floor, and to see the officials before and after the game. I travelled to Seattle University, Seattle Pacific University, and Western Washington University a couple of times. I worked very hard to advise officials to be as good as they could be. I think if you ask them, they would do just that.

I never thought that my illness would ever affect me when it came to officiating. When my body started to fail me, I felt like I lost a great love when my body was failing me to stop officiating. Everything works in mysterious ways though, and after moving to a supervisor role for many years, I am forever grateful.

We don't know how STRONG WE ARE until being strong is the ONLY CHOICE WE HAVE.
Multiple Sclerosis awareness

NCAA REGIONAL CHAMPIONSHIP
La Tech vs. USC
March 26, 1994

CHAPTER 28
Thoughts of a Good Official

A sport official's job is to make an equal playing field for the competitors. Not to lean one way or the other way, just to make it fair and equal to everybody participating.

You need to be a good communicator, know the rules, study hard, and you have to have compassion, control, and communication. The rules and mechanics of the game can come after, but you need those three qualities first to be successful.

Something the general public doesn't get to see is how much studying goes into officiating right and how hard it is to be in shape for the job. Even in my day before DVDs and such, we watched films on VCRs. We didn't get immediate feedback like the officials do now, but one of the things we all did was make sure we knew the rules.

Usually the people who make the bad calls don't know the rules. But also, anything against one team ends up seeming like the wrong call if the audience is rooting for that team.

One time while officiating at UW, we had a good crowd there, probably 5000 or 6000 people. UW was hosting Stanford, probably the biggest game at the time in the country. I made a call against UW and the crowd booed at me. I went over to the UW coach, Chris Golbrecht and she said I got the call right. It's rough hearing the stadium boo you despite doing the job justice, but it's more important to make the right call.

I'm lucky in my career that I didn't make a lot of wrong calls. Coaches liked me and fans usually liked me. It's just that Stanford is so well known in basketball and the crowd was full of people, so the game was high-stakes. I even knew some of the people who were booing me.

Generally, though, as a good official, you walk into a gym and people smile. They're glad that they'll get a fair game. Ask any coach I officiated or assigned officials for. I know I did well and I'm very proud of that. It makes me sad that I don't have that relationship all the time anymore as a supervisor, but coaches used to call after games and tell me about the calls that my officials made. They knew they'd get the truth from me. I bet you if we talked to any of the coaches I still talk to, that's what you'll hear.

One of my first conversations with Dana was my second year as a WCC official. We had dinner together and didn't talk basketball, but talked about our common issue of our parents growing old and the roles and responsibilities we now had in their lives. I walked away thinking, "How many bosses take the time to know their employees outside of their job?" I felt very special that day. I learned that real life connections to people is what Dana was about.

Another fond memory was camp at UW. After a long day Dana took some of us back to the hotel. We were laughing so hard Dana ran a red light (luckily it was late at night). We were all screaming that she was trying to kill us. This made us laugh harder. I hadn't laughed that hard in years. Dana made it great fun!!

I will always remember what you've done for me on the court, but more importantly, off the court.

– Cathi Cornell (Division 1 Women's Basketball Official)

CHAPTER 29

Camps and Start of Danaisms

I called Lynda Goodrich, my coach when I went to Western Washington, and asked if I could meet her for lunch. We did, and I told her that I had MS. I wouldn't be able to run for much longer. Instead of physical running, she suggested I run a camp, so I said good idea. My first camp was in Bellingham, Washington, where she was still the coach. I lost the ability to run after three years, but I still ran a camp for seventeen years.

11 people attended my first camp. 130 attended my last full camp. Seventeen years of camp is a pretty good gig. Prior to running camp, I had only been to the PAC-10 camp, Bob Olson's camp, and Sue Kennedy's camp in Texas, so it felt like I was starting fresh. There were four of us: Joe Jarvie, Woody Woodruff, Michelle Duncan, and me. They know how and where it all began. In our first camp, we all slept in the dorm and Michelle needed to bring her young children. They watched TV while we worked.

One famous Danaism began here. "Who is a lead, raise your hand!" I knew as camp director I wanted to teach leadership on the court! There are many other Danaisms, but that was the first and it stayed through for 25 camps and 17 years.

I ranged from 1 camp a summer to doing 2 to 3 camps per year as a director. Over time, they all became too much and I began only one large camp at the University of Washington. I couldn't have done a camp without my incredible staff. Penny Davis became a leader in the classroom, so she naturally became my first lieutenant at the West Coast camps. Many thanks to the staffers who helped at me run camps at Pepperdine, Portland, San Diego, and Washington. 25 camps total and

I couldn't even walk at the last 10 years of my camps. My staff included Joe Thompson, Penny Davis, Karen Lasuik, Carla Fujimoto, Lisa Ulmer, Tom Dubus, Anita Myles, Wanda Szeremeta, and Jay Schumacher. I had many staffers, but these names followed me wherever I go! I only did the Pepperdine Camp one year. That was one of the years I did three camps in one summer. So, again, I was walking with a cane at that time. The thing about camp in Malibu in the summer, is the Pacific Coast Highway, the road from LA to Malibu, was closed. So we needed to get a hotel on the other side of the mountains from Malibu. As we came from the hotel to Malibu, when you come over the mountains, you get to see the ocean over there, it's so beautiful. What I enjoyed about the camp was the different location. It was only the one year, but every coach in the WCC wanted me to run a camp at their school because they had free referees for their camp. I didn't charge the schools anything for doing a camp at their school so all the coaches knew it would be a good camp and got free referees for their camp.

I think I did camp at four of the eight schools. I got asked every year by all of the coaches in the conference. Even though UW wasn't in the conference, I did a camp there. I didn't have to travel so I could do it from my home. Their facilities had five floors available while most schools don't have that many floors going at once. I could have more campers because of five floors with three officials on each floor. Fifteen officials could work each hour. All the campers could get five games during the length of the camp.

The only thing different at Pepperdine Camp was the outside courts. This is the one and only time and I let the campers wear shorts.

The reason I didn't let them wear shorts was I didn't want to see black shoes with white socks, nor their knobby knees, or knee brace! Wearing pants had no distractions. I didn't look at anything other than their officiating. So I wanted them in full gear while they refereed without any distraction. I had them wear my camp shirts when they weren't officiating because all the girls playing in the camp could see what they could do even when they were done playing.

I had one player at Loyola tell her coach that she wanted to learn how to referee. I always offered free scholarships to any ex-players who wanted to come to camp. Taryn came to camp four years and then I hired her for the WCC. It was exciting to watch a player become a referee and then a referee in the conference. Overall, I must have allowed just over a dozen players join this way.

I expected a full uniform at camp and a camp shirt when they weren't refereeing. Really my biggest rule was don't be late for meetings and don't be late for your game. If someone came late to the initial first meeting, I would stop speaking and I would have all the campers turn around and look at the person. I wouldn't say anything. My staff didn't like that I did that, but I wanted everyone to know the importance of being on time during a meeting or a game. My staff gave me a bad time, but the campers knew they needed to wear their shirts and they knew not to be late. Those rules preceded me and they knew before they came into camp.

There was one time I invited a gentleman to be a staffer. He showed up in cut-off shorts and a shirt with holes in it. I told him that you don't set an example like that. He asked why not? So I told him to just go home. My philosophy was to set an example for my staff, and campers. Every year I gave my staff new polo shirts and new things to wear; those staffers who worked every year probably had at least ten different shirts from each year. I treated my staff really well, but they needed to lead by example. Sending that staffer home was the appropriate thing to do.

I always lead by example to my staff. I was never late. I always dressed appropriately. My staff knew that and respected that. And so when somebody didn't, that was unacceptable and they knew it.

One of the times I went to Pepperdine as a supervisor, one of my referees who I saw going to the game, and she had red fingernail polish on. I asked if she had fingernail polish remover because I wanted her to take it off. Every little detail is a distraction, and people will notice. So take it off so people won't focus on your nails instead of your refereeing. That is a perfect example of my referees leading by example. She told everybody I did that and there is nobody I know to this day who would wear bright fingernail polish to each game.

I had so many campers come more than one year. On the average, campers would come about three years, even if they got hired in division one.

I didn't raise my price for my campers even though all of the other camps were going way up to $450-$500. The max I charged was $350, but in 17 years of running my camp I only raised the camp price once. I wasn't in it for money, but I did have to pay for my staff and everything else.

The way to move up as a basketball official, first and foremost, is to do a good job at whatever level you're at. You need to be noticed by somebody who supervises the next level up. One of the biggest thrills I got out of running my camp was watching officials and offering them a contract to work a higher level. I did 25 camps in 17 years and I probably hired in my time at least 300 officials. And I got such a thrill seeing them when I could hire them to division one or division two. But you have to go to camps and you have to be willing to get better. You can't just go to camps and be seen, you also have to be skilled enough to move up.

With the internet now, you can just go online and look up a referee camp and fifty or so will pop up. When I started in division one, you just had to hear about them from somebody else. There were very few camps and the very first camps I went to, you didn't know what to expect because there were not many camps around. It was Lynda's idea to run a camp. I didn't know how to run a camp for the life of me, but I tried and seventeen years later, 25 camps.

I loved doing camps and the staff backed me up. The first eight years, I did everything myself. Every classroom. The last 9 years—I called them my Lieutenants—I told them to take care of certain parts of camp and I took care of others. The most fun I had was buying the shirts and jackets I was going to give my staff as presents.

My conference, the WCC, we were known as the hugging conference because we really liked each other and I made every effort we could to have a good staff of people who liked each other.

Everything I did, I just did it my way. The truth is I didn't learn it from anybody else. There weren't many camps before mine, and certainly none taken in the direction I took it. When I say I did it my way it's because I really didn't have a mentor to run camps so the main things that I would teach for my campers besides the X's and O's on the floor professionalism dress great, how to shake somebody's hand to represent yourself when you come to the gym, and how to believe in yourself while carrying integrity. Compassion, control, and communication my 3 C's.

I would often talk to my staff about how they dressed acted on the floor. Integrity, professionalism, compassion, and communication were the most important pieces even for the staff, to stand-out. I truly believe perception is reality and think these were the things that were most important to me. This is how I ran my camps and this is how I ran my conferences and I wished them all nothing but success.

CHAPTER 30
#1 & #2 Officials

I love all of my officials, but Penny and Karen are like daughters to me. I didn't have any of my own kids. The joke was that Penny was my #1 and Karen was my #2. They never got anything they didn't earn, but they were family to me.

They were both campers, both officials moving from campers to division one officials, and they both became staff at my camp. They worked the whole system from campers to conference officials. They both got to work the tournament, they both got to work the NCAA, Penny was the alternate at the final four and Karen went to the Olympics. I got to watch the two of them grow up and become phenomenal people and phenomenal officials. They're definitely like daughters to me, I opened the door, but they walked through.it Having Karen go to the Olympics knowing I taught her some of her officiating skills, meant a lot to me.

Penny going on to be an alternate for the women's final four and working conference tournament finals also ranks up there. I think I've had a big part in her development. She runs camps herself, so I'm guessing she takes a little bit of my stuff to her camp. I enjoy seeing how my "kids" grow after leaving my camps. They represent my proudest moments.

Penny Davis, (division one official, camp director)

Well, first a little background on me, I started officiating in 1997. I played basketball in high school and college and wanted to be involved, so I went out on a limb and looked up a high school association because I loved the game. During my first year, people saw I had a lot of potential and they told me I needed to go to a camp. I didn't know what that meant, but the first camp I went to was Dana's camp in Portland. During that first year, I kept hearing her name around camp. Dana, Dana, Dana. It was clear she was a person who had a lot of influence and that she held a position of power and respect. It was kind of like Madonna or Obama where she didn't need a last name. She had that rhetoric. Everybody knew who you were talking about if you said Dana. I had her in my mind on a big pedestal. When I started officiating, it was like I got bitten by the bug, and I just wanted to go as high as I could. She acted as a gatekeeper for officiating, being the barrier between starting out and getting to the next level.

She grasped onto me and kind of knew I was going places. I didn't know at the time that she had been diagnosed with MS, so I wasn't aware of that backstory. Looking back, I think that she saw me as a way to be back on the court. I became the golden child in a lot of people's minds and she always had a special affinity towards me, and it went both ways because she definitely helped me and gave me a lot of opportunities, occasionally before I was ready. I was a teacher's pet and probably her favorite student, so to speak.

Dana pushed me early on, and I became a staff member. She put me in a position to be in the front of the room. I'm not in teaching, communication, or sales. I'm an IT person. I get along fine with my computer; she challenged me and tested me to be in front of people and to go over public speaking. I experienced an evolution and growth that had nothing to do with officiating.

I've been running my own camps for about 10 years now, so speaking doesn't give me as much trepidation now. I don't think I'd be this far if she hadn't been pushing me that way. I see a lot of it coming full circle. In the last few years it was pretty amazing seeing her going through the camp settings with her disease. She had to show a lot of humility. Previously she was able to stand, then she went to a cane, and then she needed her scooter. She's done this in a setting where we need to show a lot of strength and courage. What she has to do through her illness is more challenging than any game I've ever refereed. To get through the fatigue and everything we cannot understand, we can't even imagine it with all of the things she's lost.

There was definitely a little bit of the fear factor and not knowing going into Dana's camp. I was 22 years old in that environment with no idea of what to expect on what would come. I only had my perception of things I had heard and her reputation that she formulated in my mind. She certainly had her way of pushing people's limits, not in a drill sergeant way, but finding that soft spot and digging into it a little bit to help everybody grow. Advancing in officiating and getting that division one contract is very competitive. There are a lot of people in camp that I can say she played some favorites, but some people thought that she didn't favor them. There was some difference of opinion based on who you were or where you were from. There was a component where some people thought there was injustice.

I think my favorite story was when we had a big 50th birthday party for Dana. This was at the Double Tree Hotel. All cars had to be self-parked or parked by valet. She could drive her mobility van and scooter into it. It still had regular foot controls, but it had hand controls as well to accommodate Dana. Dana had the absolute best day. She'd been roasted, cheered, and treated, it was a great celebration. The valet driver was pulling out the cars. We see Dana's van being pulled up, and know this is a van that is out of control. The van driver struck the center landscape area in the roundabout at the Double Tree. I started freaking out because I knew it was her car. I asked, "What are you doing?" and he said, "I didn't know how to drive with the hand controls!"

The three or four of us tried to find her insurance information, but we couldn't find the paperwork in her vehicle. We realized we had to tell Dana in the middle of this celebration. As the 'Golden Child' and her kid, I volunteered to go tell her. I took the key out from her scooter and pushed them out of her reach. I knew if she learned what was going on, shit would hit the fan and she would storm out.

I said, "Hey Dana, something happened to your vehicle..." I knew it would cause stress and I didn't want to give her that added stress of knowing her mobility would be hindered. I knew this could be a souring point in her night, so had to tell her about the incident delicately. To do that, I took her keys away. The rabbit speed.

Another memory involves one of Dana's camp policies. At the camps, one of her pet peeves had a lot to do with guys with facial hair. That's a no go in officiating. She would be the first to tell somebody you're coming to camp, this isn't that kind of environment, you need a haircut and can't represent people in officiating with facial hair. Day two or day three of camp, they would be clean shaven and you wouldn't recognize them from day one or day two. One guy from Alaska mentioned he didn't know what would happen when he went home to see his wife, but they were willing to go the distance to make that impression.

She had us yell "be a lead" as a little chant. She wanted to promote confidence and leadership. She would also have everybody introduce themselves and she would shake hands with everyone. If they had a soft handshake, she would call you out and make a comment. To close camp, everybody would do this little speech about what they learned. Over the years, it became a kumbaya session. It felt like church to some degree. People would come up and give a testimony; there would be tears, hugs, and concessions. It became an emotional spirit because people's vulnerabilities came forth and we all experienced personal growth in some form. It would be pretty emotional and humbling for people, but ultimately pretty good even though the closing sessions could last a couple of hours. Those sessions were pretty interesting...

For my camp, I did follow this format initially, although I shied away from that aspect, but there are a lot of elements in my camp that I took from hers. I took elements from all of the camps I went to, but there are certainly Dana's marks throughout.

I think Dana tried to keep MS away, and she fought tooth and nail every step from walking to walking with a cane. When I first met her, she walked with a little limp, but I didn't know what was up. Then it progressed with a cane, but she had to fall down I don't know how many times before she got a cane. If I'm not mistaken, she had a walker briefly too. She was very prideful.

I remember she drove this red Honda that had a weird crane that would put her scooter in the trunk and for her to drive that sporty car and have that image, nobody could see her MS while she was in her car. It came to the point that she definitely needed her mobility van. She couldn't do all the work with the scooter in the trunk and the crane. I remember going with her to the mobility van place to try to sell her on the idea of getting a van. I told her she was doing things much too hard. She struggled with the image side. Nobody from the officiating standpoint saw MS as, "wow she can't do her job" we saw it more as, "wow this is a shitty hand to be dealt." I've seen people with terminal illnesses handle them differently and with a different attitude than Dana. Part of it is that her family support is somewhat limited, her parents have both passed, and her network of friends is pretty small. There are a lot of officials who posed as being her friends because of what they perceived she could give them. I think as she moved away from officiating, that network diminished a little further.

I've been there with a lot of moments with Dana, whether it is the end of a relationship or we couldn't find a room available. I've said, "Hey we'll make this work," and I've pulled a mattress off of the bed so she could get in. I put a spin on it and told her we'd make it work.

A lot of emotions come to me when I think of Dana. I smile a lot because the first thing that comes to mind is "mullet" and it's kind of weird. But we've had a lot of conversations about her hair and she is in complete mullet denial. Any time she gets it cut I make a comment because that's the first thing that comes to mind.

During one of my camps early on as a supervisor, Penny Davis came up to me. She told me she was ready for division one, but I knew it would be better for her to wait one more year. She was pissed off at the time, but later in our relationship she thanked me more times than I can count for that one extra year. I always tell officials it's easier to get in than stay in. She's done many, many conference championships, and she is doing incredibly well, also running her own camps. I am so excited that I have been her teacher, and now her friend and that she is carrying on my legacy.

CHAPTER 31
Getting Equality as New Supervisor

Tim Moser (U of Alaska head women's basketball coach, assistant coach Colorado state)

With over twenty-five years of experience, I have worked hand and hand with officials and directors of officials. Dana Senders was a true professional. She was always there to both listen to and gather thoughts and ideas from head coaches. I enjoyed my time working with her because she always cared enough to hear me out and take the time to see from a coach's perspective. I gained so much respect from her during my time working with her and I know that everything she did was for the fairness of the game. Most importantly, I trusted her decisions and her feedback.

So you probably want to know how I got started as the supervisor of the West Coast Conference. I was at the last game at the WCC conference tournament observing the game for Dean Crowley, the supervisor at that time was at the men's tournament. I was up in the bleachers when the commissioner of the West Coast Conference, Mike Gillerand, sat down next to me. He asked me if I would consider being the supervisor of women's officials for the West Coast Conference. I had already been NCAA assistant coordinator. I said absolutely I would consider that.

I called Marcy to ask her what she thought. We didn't know how long the assistant job was going to be available. So I called Mike and told him I would take the job. This was a great opportunity for me since I couldn't referee anymore and I loved the conference. I have great connections with the coaches and athletic directors, I was familiar where all the schools were, and, at the time, I was still walking, although my left leg was not working well. I was able to get around to the schools no problem. It was a dream job because I could still be a part of officiating and this way I had an impact on the growth of the conference schools.

When I took over as supervisor, there was quite a discrepancy between the officials for the men's games and the officials for the women's games. The men's officials got more travels than the women's side did and the pay was different for the men's officials than for the women's. I started as supervisor by getting equality for the women's basketball side. It only took two years with committees and the coaches to figure out a way to get the travels to balance out to be the same on the woman's side and the men's side. It only took two years for the pay to become equal on both sides. So at this time we had limited travels because of the expense of the conference. I then had to keep the coaches happy by seeing as many officials as they could and keep my budget in line on how many travels we used. So I spent the next years working hard to get the travels up so I could keep the coaches and officials happy while getting the pay up so that everyone would be equal on both sides of the court. By the time I left, travels were as high as they could get and the pay was equal, so I had done my job.

Mike Gilleran ~ WCC Commissioner, 1984-2008

We brought Dana Senders on board as our Supervisor of Women's Officials in 1997, and I worked with Dana until my retirement in 2008. Dana earned the respect of officials and coaches alike for her work ethic and honesty, as well as for her unwavering commitment to the improvement of officiating. Dana understood that we are in this business for the young people who play the sport, and she expected her officials to demonstrate a combination of rules expertise and common sense, just as she demonstrated when she was a top official.

I especially appreciated the fact that Dana never sought to avoid criticism or accountability. In fact, coaches typically told me they really respected Dana for her willingness to listen to their concerns and to communicate their concerns to her officials. Dana had no agenda other than to continue to make our women's officiating stronger and stronger. We were able to attract officials who could have made more money working for other conferences because of their friendship with and loyalty to Dana, and that was a huge benefit to our conference.

Nothing in college athletics administration is more of an emotional issue than officiating. As commissioner, it was great for me to have someone with Dana's experience and personality working in that volatile and sensitive area. She listened, she communicated and she taught. She was always positive and enthusiastic. She understood that officials must make instant decisions that are often unpopular, and she understood the value of communication.

Dana was a joy to work with because of her passion for what she did. Many coaches and players benefited from her wisdom and personality, whether they ever knew Dana or not, and I know I was a better commissioner because of Dana's efforts.

CHAPTER 32

Becoming a Better Speaker.
What I Loved About Camp

The first camp I spoke at other than my own was a high school camp in Kirkland, Washington. Penny Davis asked me to speak, and I watched Penny since she started officiating. She wasn't at camp to help me know the crowd, but I talked to everyone like they were my Campers. I tried to make them leaders and to find out why they were refereeing.

These were not this kind of motivated officials. They came to camp to socialize, but I tried to get the most out of them. I saw a lot of potential in one official, Stacy Brodzik, but she really didn't want to talk to me. I asked her why she refereed, but she simply wanted to be with her friends and have fun. She didn't have any goals beyond high school officiating. However, the next year she came to my camp like I lit a fire in her. In a few years, she worked division two basketball and wanted a division one, I gave her a game at Seattle University so she could at least have the experience of working at that level. I know she's grateful for what I did for her.

I never forget how the campers acted when I first spoke. The next year when I spoke, the campers were more aware of their motivation.

Penny told me I needed to get a van with hand controls instead of my sporty Honda because I couldn't drive in a car anymore. She took me out to Woodinville to drive a ramp vehicle. A Chevy. I never liked Chevy until I bought that van, and I loved it for 8 years. I needed the hand controls and I needed a ramp van. I really didn't want to do it, but it's one of the best things that I ever did I thank Penny for that. She's always been there for me.

By 1999, I was walking with a cane. During a staff meeting at the Pepperdine Camp one night, the security guard came in and asked who was in charge because of a situation over at one of the dorm rooms. One of your group stole a pizza from the kids. We walked over to the dorm room to investigate, even though the walking distance challenged me.

When I walked in the door, everybody started singing happy birthday to me.it was August 8th which was my birthday. It was a nice thought, but the noise was loud and I needed them to stop so I could see if they stole a pizza from the kids. The pizza guy offered it to them because whoever ordered it wasn't around to pay. They didn't steal it, all is forgiven, and off we went to our hotel to wake up in six hours to start the next day.

During my camp I would sit between two courts on the University of Washington main floor. Officials would line up to speak with me. Penny thought we should have one of those ticket dispensers used at delis so they could take a number, stand in line, and I would call out a number for the next person. Although I thought that was funny, we never did take numbers.

I loved every minute of it. Talking with everybody at camp was special. The best part of it was telling people I hired them to Division one or Division two and seeing that they were so happy to work. Their reactions were awesome but sometimes I didn't want them to tell anyone until the end of camp. Even though that was hard for them, they did just that. I didn't want anybody to be jealous of the campers I hired.

At one of my camps in Portland, I was on the baseline watching officials. Every time one of the referees went by, I caught a very strong scent of flowers. I figured out it was Cathi Cornell and I told her I was considering hiring her that year for the WCC, but her perfume (or whatever it was) was too strong. I told her not to wear so much because the aroma was distracting. I'm sure Cathi remembers and I hired her at that camp for the next season. She told me later that it was the third day of camp and she wanted to have a decent smell, after running 3 days might have a different aroma. It was a lesson learned for both of us. Same camp I was walking with a cane and I was on the Baseline and

I slipped and fell even with my cane. Three of the officials ran over to make sure I was okay and I was more embarrassed than hurt so I said I'm okay go back to what you were doing. I just didn't want to show any weakness I guess that was a weakness in itself.

After hiring Cathi, she eventually became a member of my camp staff. I was proud to have her join my team.

I did three camps over this summer: Seattle, Portland, and San Diego. It was tiring and hard on me but I got it all done walking with a cane. With my whole staff working over three camps, it was one of my more grueling summers, but one of the most productive as well. My team was as tired as me, but I know from the number of people hired and the education given that summer that the benefits outweighed my exhaustion.

As you heard early on about my 50th birthday, I decided to have a big party for myself. There was a buffet and a bar. We started by showing my elite 8 basketball games on the big screen. Annette Tracy was the MC for the birthday party and it turned into a roast for me. I'd never been roasted before, but 70 people there took turns on calling some people up, all of them thinking of different things to roast me about . I had to contact the valet office to get their insurance company after my van was driven into the rocks.

My good friends Jill and Iris were there along with many other people from all aspects of my life: my doctor, basketball, softball friends, and my sister Diane. I have to say that was the best night of my life, besides the car troubles. My insurance fixed it and it was still drivable but turning 50 and the regional finals were the best nights of my life.

Gordon Presnell ~ (Seattle Pacific University) Boise State Women's Basketball Coach:

I had the opportunity to work with Dana, when she served as the supervisor of officials for the conference I was coaching in. I found her to have a passion for basketball, a love for the craft of officiating, and a thorough understanding and interpretation of the rules. She was always forthright, organized, transparent and operated out of complete integrity."

When Dana was an official, I recall as a young coach having her in a game of mine, and really giving her a hard time. I complained about everything. Then about a week later, I went as a fan to the biggest game in the country at that time; The University of Washington versus Stanford. Dana was officiating. At that moment I realized how talented of an official she was and maybe in the future I should just sit down and coach my team!

CHAPTER 33

My Vocation Even with MS

I saw an ad for novelty sports sales person. I faxed my resume to them at 1 o'clock and they called back at 1:30 and this was on a Monday. On Tuesday, I went in for an interview. I asked if there was anything else I could do. They said, "we'll call you." Two days after my interview, I saw Pacific Direct had called on my caller ID, so I hit redial and it called my future manager. She asked how I got her number and I told her. She said she called to offer me a job. It's Thursday now. I told her I could start Monday. So on Monday I went in there in my scooter, even though I walked to my interview with my cane. This was a day of transitions.

It was my first day working there so I was pretty excited about that. I became their number one salesperson at the company's highest level. They had 35 employees. 6 years later when the company went out of business, it went from 35 to 25 to 10 employees, and then my boss and a warehouse person accountant were all that remained. Besides myself.

The company went out of business the same year that I got fired from supervisor of the West Coast Conference, so I knew that summer would be my last camp. I didn't know where my job was heading so I applied for disability. Normally people get denied on their first application, but I hired a disability lawyer for $500 and I was accepted for disability on the first try. I worked really hard on jobs all my life, but within six months I started getting my disability check.

Kelli Lindley, Northwest Nazarene University Director of Athletics

"During my time as the Head Women's Basketball Coach at Northwest Nazarene University, I always appreciated how approachable and sincere Dana was whenever I had a concern or question. These conversations led to a friendship with Dana and it was always clear she cared deeply for the team she led and the many coaches and staff she worked with. Dana's work ethic and commitment to excellence was a great example for me and I thoroughly enjoyed partnering with her in the world of college athletics."

CHAPTER 34
Losing My Parents

My brother Roger moved my parents closer to him in Los Angeles for their Fight For Life. They needed to be in warmer weather. My parents meant a lot to me, so going from seeing them at least once a month in Seattle to calling them once a month had a big impact.

I got a call from my brother. If I wanted to see mom, I needed to get down to LA right away. My father was suffering greatly from dementia, so we were worried about him, but my mother was in the hospital after her intestine had blown a whole in it. My mom had rheumatoid arthritis, an autoimmune disease which MS is also. So I arrived in my scooter, not aware of anything, her eyes were closed. The doctors gave her a very short amount of time to live so they gave us one option: they had to do surgery to see if they could repair her intestine. If they were in there for longer than thirty minutes, that would be a good sign for us. If they came out before that, then that means the surgery would have no chance of success.

They returned after about twenty minutes Her intestine was not reparable. We took my mom back to her room in the ICU, took the breathing tube out, and they said she would pass away shortly. If anyone ever wondered where I get my stubbornness, it's from my mom. They took the breathing tube out and it took four hours for her to take her last breath. She was there, but my brother left to take care of my dad after all that then my mom started to have trouble breathing. Mom and I were the only two in the room. The weirdest part about this whole thing was my mom's eyes opening like you wouldn't believe. My brother came in and I was crying. I thought she woke up. They never told me this could happen. My brother comforted mom as well as me. Roger and I watched her take her last breath. This was a new experience for me, witnessing a final breath, her eyes closed and I was bawling. We sat with her for a few minutes. I was very close to my mom, so this was very hard on me.

I went back to Seattle and kept working my jobs, but fast forward a few years later and my brother called me and said that I needed to come see my dad. I couldn't watch that again. I stayed in Seattle, but my brother was with him when he passed away, 5 years later my brother Roger went up to Oregon to be with my big brother Alan as he passes at 64. By this time I could not travel alone even in my scooter, I was very close to my big brother we talked every week. He was the kind of brother that would just listen when I talked and not try to fix anything. Four years later, I moved to Los Angeles. Roger and I found out later that my older brother had cancer that had metastasized. He had very few days left to live, when we found out. So that's when Roger flew up to Oregon where my older brother lived, so was with him. So I lost both my parents and my brother Alan, all in a short span. I still have my brother Roger and my sister in Arizona, and I've been trying to develop a better relationship with them. I really wish the rest of my family were still around to help me through my life and MS, but they're in a better place.

CHAPTER 35

Showing My Emotions in Las Vegas. Getting Terminated

I had been in my scooter for I don't know how many years as supervisor. I could still stand and do my job. I went to games in my scooter without a problem. Mike Gilleran, the commissioner who hired me, hired an advisor of women's sports whom I didn't get along with, and, one year later, Mike was fired.

I worked in the conference for 12 years as a supervisor before she was hired. I knew a lot more than this new gal, but she hassled me constantly over things that my 19 years of experience with the WCC told me would work.

We needed to travel to Las Vegas for a conference tournament. The floor that the games were on was 2 inches above the main floor so I couldn't reach my seat to watch the first game without a ramp. I was more upset than I have ever been. It felt like my disability was keeping me from doing my job. The officials at the tournament saw how upset I was, they had never seen me so vulnerable. I was crying, frustrated, and didn't know what to do. Before this I had never cried in front of my officials before. A gentleman who ran the facility said he could have had a ramp for me without a problem? If somebody had told them, he would have had that done before we had come there. This upset me the most, knowing that nobody let the gym manager know what I needed and nobody I worked with seemed to care. I felt they set me up for failure. They put up a ramp in minutes, I got to my seat, and the games went on.

I don't think I showed any of my officials how hard my life was. I don't think I ever let that show. When I was crying there, in front of my officials, I think that humbled me a lot. It never crossed my mind to not show vulnerability, I just never did. Subconsciously I didn't want to show being vulnerable. When I lost it in front of all of them, I think that was the first time I had done that.

The hardest thing for me is I didn't want to show weakness while refereeing, as a supervisor, or a camp director. I saw my illness as a weakness. When I ref or work or whatever I was involved in, I just would not show weakness. An example of this, I was in the hospital one time in Seattle. I was not supposed to leave the hospital per my doctor, but Seattle U was a block from the hospital. I left the hospital in my scooter to watch the basketball game to see Penny, and to see the coach from University of Portland, Jim Sollers. I never looked in the mirror and saw weakness. I don't like looking in the mirror period. I'm so used to not thinking about things emotionally in front of people. It wasn't a conscious effort. It's really hard for me to show my emotions because at the time I just did what I had to do to keep going. I would just rise up every day. I didn't let my emotions get the best of me. I cried after a few basketball games when my legs started to go, but that wasn't in front of anybody. I moved to the next place I needed to be and kept going forward.

Back to Vegas despite the lack of coordination from the WCC office, we were able to explore the night in Las Vegas to make up for it. We saw the Jersey Boys (they played all the songs that I knew). The best part was singing along to the songs. A referee asked how I knew all the songs and I said, "they're from my era!" After that concert was over we went to one of the bars at the casino. I have a picture of me, Penny, and Karen. We sat there and it was one of those nights, I would never forget and did all that in my scooter, I just enjoyed their company and going to see the Jersey Boys and seeing it with them. It was the company with them that made the experience so enjoyable.

The final night I went to see Cher with some other officials and I had a wonderful time with them as well. At least I can say I got to know everybody that was down there for the tournament and spend some real quality time with them, not knowing at that time it would be the last division 1 tournament I would be a part of.

I went back to Seattle to do my first game at the University of Washington for the NCAA tournament as an observer, Before my first game at the University of Washington, I was asked to meet with the new commissioner of the WCC over breakfast. Before we could order any food, he said I'm not renewing your contract. Out of the blue. No option to do anything better, no option to change. I asked for one more year so I could adjust to his needs, but no luck. I found out later that he had already hired my replacement before he fired me. I called the NCAA, and they let me know that I no longer had an obligation to observe the University of Washington game. I was still upset, but I cared more about the officials than my feelings so I still observed the game after all that. Remembering still in my scooter and having to drive my van with hand controls with tears in my eyes.

I felt like I was let go for no reason. This new commissioner offered me a $6,000 stipend for walking away from the job. That wasn't good enough. I tried to look into the reason I was let go, despite my experience. The only thing I could think of was the big deal that I made about them not having a ramp, in Vegas.

I looked into my options regarding my wrongful termination, and started to make some calls. The first two attorneys I found in California where the conference office was, turned me down. The third said after talking that he really liked me so I filed a lawsuit with hiss help against the West Coast Conference, for wrongful termination.

I flew down to San Francisco for a deposition and then the next week flew back down, I plead my case to a arbitrator, and I am so glad even though physically this was so hard all I really wanted was my job back, but that wasn't going to happen. I suppose I had the satisfaction of letting the conference know that just causes are required to fire people. My disability had a lot to do with the firing, so the arbitrator was very helpful in resolving the conflict.

When I lost that job, my regular job went out of business. My illness always stayed away enough, but I couldn't fight the MS the way I used to. I loved my jobs so much that when they ended, my health got worse. My health and the jobs were connected, so losing the jobs changed my life forever. Now I'm just doing my best to fight through MS.

All thirteen years as a supervisor I walked with a cane or used a scooter. I always did my job when requested and nobody ever told me that I needed to do it differently or that the job wasn't getting done. When I had elevator access, I would go see officials after the games, and, again, I was never told that I was not doing a great job with the officials.

I loved officiating, I loved supervising, I loved running camps, I loved teaching young officials. My work kept me in the state of wellness I needed to continue working.

CHAPTER 36

Being a Supervisor, Camp Director, with a Chronic Illness

From 1997 to 2011, I Supervised the West Coast Conference Division one, The Great Northwest Athletic Conference Division two, and the Northwest Conference Division three. I went to all my games, handled all West Coast officials, and did all West Coast tournaments.

I traveled to many schools during my tenure as supervisor of officials—San Diego, Portland, Santa Clara, Gonzaga, USF, Loyola, Pepperdine, and St. Mary's, all eight schools. When needed, I observed the NCAA tournament as a supervisor, including at Santa Barbara, the University of Washington, and Portland State University. I also attended a Regional as an observer in Norman, Oklahoma with my friend Kaye Garms, the supervisor of the Western Athletic Conference. We stayed the full four days to see every official. Kaye was the supervisor who hired me as an official in the Western Athletic Conference and we became friends partially because we were seated alphabetically at supervisor meetings in Indiana and were always next to each other.

I spent 35 years in basketball officiating, 20 years on the court, 15 years off. I know I went through the door of gyms well over 1000 times, and worked in 32 different states. Whether as an official, as a supervisor, or as a camp director, I would just rise up and do what had to be done no matter what the day brought for me. I learned from those before me and developed what my staff would fondly call

"Danaisms". To this day, "be a lead" is being used somewhere! I want to be remembered for doing everything in my own way.

I lived my avocation my way, not necessarily because it was the only way, but because there were not too many officiating camps before mine, particularly ones that I attended. So I really didn't have a mentor figure on how to run camps. I focused on teaching campers my priorities: professionalism and integrity. Any place can teach the X's and O's of officiating, but teaching compassion, control, and competence, as a person transcends those lessons in importance. If you enter an officiating space without professionalism, then your calls may not be taken with the seriousness you need. If you enter a space without personal integrity and the ability to commit to and believe in every call you make, then your calls may be, in turn, called into question. You can make all of the right calls, but without integrity and professionalism, the crowd may not be sold on those calls. Officials are in the business of sales: selling their calls. This begins with how you speak, act, shake hands, dress, and carry yourself. This is how I ran camps and how I ran conferences, and how I officiated. Everybody learned the importance of appearing on court as a professional and I wish my campers and officials nothing but success.

When I was 33 years old I started to think of how to manage money for my future, the same year I was diagnosed with MS. I was very fortunate that I found the right broker to help me get started with my IRA money. This money grows and, you can convert it to a Roth IRA which is what I did. I didn't expect to be spending my retirement money so soon, but I am grateful I saved ahead of time.

The biggest piece of advice that I could give is that life is like a box of chocolates you never know what you're going to get. I know that's a Forrest Gump movie saying but it's the truth, especially for me with my MS. You just don't know what you're going to get every day. This has been a great asset to me in my life and it grew over all those years of running camps, working two jobs, and keeping my sales jobs. So if you can save 20 bucks a week towards a retirement fund what I would suggest to anyone whether you're thirty, forty, fifty, or whatever age you are, this is a great piece of education. But this is something that I would like to teach on to all of you so if you managed to pick that up out of my story, I will be forever grateful.

One of the things I did to keep working hired a trainer to my house twice a week work with my legs and my arms to keep me strong enough to do my job Peggy lived very close to continue to help me keep strength in my legs hoping that someday to be able to walk again. She was a believer in keeping my strength long as I could when I moved to California when I retired I lost strength in my legs because I didn't have her a train meant a great deal of my strength was her belief in me.

Peggy McCartney, Athletic Trainer

I met Dana on the phone. She had called the local premier athletic club to inquire about a personal trainer to work with her. God picked me!

Dana needed some assistance to maintain her body strength with hopes of walking again. I saw Dana's primary goal was to maintain her independence. Initially, she went swimming and to yoga, as well as additionally using her upper arm ergometer as often as she could. I focused on strength, flexibility and having fun! Smiles and laughter is always good medicine.

Dana is strong and determined. She worked out hard every time we met. We mainly used resistance bands, hand weights, ankle/ wrist weights, as well as her body weight and my pressure as resistance.

I tried to do a different routine of exercises each visit- but getting all muscle groups worked. Dana has an adventurous spirit and will seek out and try new therapies, as long as her Dr. was on board. She had several sessions at a special muscle stimulation and rotation facility to help her muscle memory to stand, bike and walk. Dana worked hard to keep herself in the best condition possible. She now lives in California, and I live in Washington. We continue our friendship now with calls, texts, pictures and emails.

CHAPTER 37

Final Thoughts on Running Camps, Locker Rooms for Women, Living with MS

My camps are truly what kept my love of life going. During an average camp day, staffers would always go out on the court and talk to campers. Usually I would have enough staffers that I would have some at the end of each court. We would help them get in position. My philosophy is that if you are at the right angle to see a play then you can get the right call. At my first camp I did a lot of that. I stood at the end and moved the officials around. As the years went on, I let my lieutenants do more of the teaching. I started the camps and I would end the camps still though.

I started telling my officials that officiating is about selling your call. If you do not believe the call you make, then nobody is going to believe it. When you blow your whistle, believe that you made the right decision. I would talk to my campers about perception, believability, and selling their perception on a situation. At my last camp I said I would play a game, I said at the beginning. I bring two campers at the front. I give two staffers half the room and I give the rest the other. How many camps did I run, how many years? So I wanted them to know my devotion to the game. I had done so many camps, so obviously I truly cared about what I was doing.

I would always break it out so my staff could talk about something. They would have responsibilities. So I would assign different parts of the education process so my staff would get education as well as the campers.

Three-day camps: Friday, Saturday, Sunday. That's how long that the kids playing in the camp could go so that's how long my referee portion would run. Sometimes we would start Thursday night with a staff meeting so starting Friday, Saturday would be games and Sunday morning would be a few games, and we would end the camp at Sunday at about 1'o'clock. At the end of my camps, all of my staffers would get up in front of the campers and say something. What they learned or what they wanted to teach or what they saw. Each one of them had to do that. I remember a camp at U of San Diego a coach was yelling at one of my staff and a camper, I said if you stop yelling I am in charge I will talk to you. Just how I did to the LA tech coach when I was officiating. The coach cooled down and the USD assistant said to me that was amazing what you just did. A learning experience for all.

Pre-games, you go through all the new rules. You go through certain positioning. You would only work with the same partner once or twice during the year. You would go over the coaches, the types of coaches you had, how you would handle them. Sometimes you would have a partner that knew the coaches so you would know the best way to talk to them.

I was working a game at the University of Portland. Men had their own locker room, but they didn't have a women's locker room. I dressed over in the room where they kept the chairs. I came to meet my partner for the first time, and I was the head official on the game. We're starting the pregame and he tells me right off the bat that he doesn't have a college jacket, but he has an NBA jacket because he was in the NBA for one year. I told him we wouldn't wear any jacket out there. He says he always wore his NBA jacket and I told him not tonight, no jackets if you don't have the right one. I could tell a woman being in charge bothered him.

As a supervisor, I would get in before the game, sit in on the pregame, and listen, I would take notes during the game, and, after the game, I would talk to officials about some of their calls. I would track their calls based on their position on the floor. Some officials would only make calls from the lead position or they would call too many calls against one of the teams and not both of the teams. Perception is everything, so if they are making calls against only one team, then what's the perception? After the game, I would either go back to my hotel or, usually when I travelled, I tried to go when there were tournaments so I could watch 12 officials in two days. That would be four games. As a supervisor, there were always three on the floor.

I often had coaches stare at me when officials made calls. A few times when I sat at the table, they would sit on the table, ask what I thought of that, and I wouldn't say anything, nor even look at them. I never talked to officials at halftime because I never wanted to make or influence on how they officiated during the game. I didn't want to impact the game or the officials. I wanted them to be consistent during the game. Consistency: they had to call it how they would call it and I didn't want to influence that.

For division two or three if we had to drive, I would still have to eat about four hours before. I would always go home after the game. I would never go out after a small college game because I had to work the next day.

I ignored having MS the best I could and, honestly, and I cannot figure out how I did 25 camps, ten years in a scooter, and go to all those games that way as a supervisor. I cannot put it together. But I think I did it because I ignored my illness. Once I wasn't doing that stuff anymore three years ago, my illness hit me in the face. It's like I had ignored it, but of course I had it, I couldn't walk, but I just got up every day, and did my work. I honestly don't know how I did it. Maybe Penny or Karen can explain what they saw, because I can't. I never talked about my illness to anybody. I'm sitting here right now shaking my head asking how the hell did I do that. If I had to guess, it was because I loved it so much. So as a supervisor I got to keep that passion. That passion said "okay MS you aren't going to attack this girl." Then when I lost it, over the last three years, it's all caught up to me. I've been in the hospital a lot over the last two years.

I have to be grateful that I've gotten to do a lot of things in my life. I'm pissed at the world that I can't do any of that stuff anymore, but I'm grateful for the many things I got to do and I didn't even realize how much I got to do until I started putting this together. I like to have answers.

My life always involved persevering through pain. I don't know what got me through all the pain and illness, but if I were to guess, it would just be an intrinsic desire to be successful and enjoy life. I know a lot of people have said, "I don't know how you did what you did" and I don't know either. The last ten years I couldn't walk so I did all my jobs on my scooter. I took my scooter and flew around the country. I even went so fast one time around the corner that I tipped my scooter and me completely over. It didn't bother me too much cuz I wasn't hurt and these two people at the airport just came up and said you need some help and they set me up and off I went.

I just loved so much what I did so much that I wasn't going to let anything stop me, and I would say that's how I got through MS. The 20 years I officiated on the court I only missed one basketball game, and I even tried to go to that one. It was a high school game and I was sick with the flu. When I got out of bed, I fell over. That was the only game that I ever missed.

I never missed work at my vocation either. I like to work, I like to do what I did, I like to be busy, and I wasn't going to let anything stop me from that. It stops me now. For the first time in my life, it stops me now, and I need to give in to something. It is very difficult to me.

It's not something I thought about at the time though. I got up and did what I love to do—what I have to do—everyday. I just did it. MS is one thing, but a sore ankle or a sore arm, you can kind of go through. But MS isn't that forgiving. Even though I tried and tried and tried. Once I got fired from my supervisor job, it was almost like finding out I'd tried hard enough. Like the world telling me it was okay that I couldn't go through it. Even today I don't like doing it, but you have to let go at some point. I can tell you that I cried after some games, but I never cried because I did a bad job, I cried because it was really hard. I truly think that my job kept my MS from getting me as bad as it has now.

It's really one answer: it stopped me from thinking about being sick. I didn't think about it. I just got up every day, did what I needed to do, got up, and I didn't even think about the fact that it was hard. I just did it. There were days I had to fight to get through. Something bigger than me got me through. Some of my friends would say a higher power helped me through it.

My advice for people with multiple sclerosis is that there is so much available for people diagnosed now. Study all of the medications and find one that works best for you. There wasn't much available when I was diagnosed. There is such a range of medications offered now. Talk to your neurologist. There is so much you can learn out there! That would be my advice.

Up until now, I was really positive and you have to stay positive for MS. You need to have passion about something else. MS stayed away from me because I was so passionate about other things in my life. Find a passion! Perseverance is about the best connection I can think of. Loving what you do and being loved by what you do are what kept my MS away from so long. My vocation and my avocation both made it easy to stay in the moment. I struggle now because I am not in the moment of any passion

Ask for a legacy, I think of all of the officials I have led. The last year I was a supervisor, I had 130 people working for me. When they think of how they learned or about whatever I was to them, I hope they think good things. That's what a legacy is. Marcy Weston is a legacy because she is the only person I know who could sit on top of the fence and please people from both sides. No matter which side of the fence you were on, you didn't feel bad walking away because of Marcy. She was so talented at that, she was spectacular. She's in the hall of fame because of that. I don't' want to be forgotten and right now I feel I have been. I don't know if I have a legacy.

A good official is a salesperson. Not just making the right calls, but believing the right calls and selling those calls. I got along with coaches so well because I made the right calls and they believed it was the right call as well.

I told a few stories to a couple of people including my brother and they all said I should write a book. You have done so much that they told me I should write a book. Originally when I started this process, I thought it would be a list of all of these stories. I thought everybody would be interested in all of these stories. It kind of blossomed into being a lot more than I thought it would be. I've done a lot of things in my long life. Originally too, I wanted people to really know what it was like before them.

I don't think officials know how little money we made, how few women officials there, were and how we were treated differently as women officials. So I think my main goal in writing was to show what it was like before and the progress made since then. That prompted me to do this.

I wanted to share to all people, but as I started telling the story, softball, officiating, supervising or living with a chronic illness. Also, anybody who would like to know how life was back in the 80's and trying to be successful at all. Athletes, coaches, officials, and anyone that has a passion in life.

Marcy Weston ~ National Coordinator of Women's Basketball Officiating (retired):

I saw Dana Senders referee a televised women's game in 1990 and was immediately impressed with her ability to manage the game, interpret & apply the game rules as written.

When Dana was recommended to officiate the NCAA tournament by the Coordinators of Officiating in the conferences she worked, I was confident Dana could work at the national level. I assigned Dana to several NCAA tournaments, up to and including a Regional Final game in 1995.

When a health situation took Dana off the court, she made a very effective transition into managing her position of Coordinator of Officiating for the West Coast Conference.

Dana also was a lauded Officiating Camp Director, giving hundreds of officials the training to mature and excel at the collegiate level. Many of her "trainees" went on to referee in NCAA & NAIA tournaments. One of her protégées worked FIBA games, culminating in an Olympic assignment in 2016.

Dana Senders is one of our finest NCAA officials and to this day is a top educator, mentor, and advisor to officials.

I have lived, been loved, fallen down and pulled myself up. My life has had joy and sadness. Through it all friends have come and gone, but my referee, family will be part of my life forever. Getting MS changed my life I have to say not in a direction I would have chosen but allowed me to become a teacher that touched many lives, and touched my heart.